Baptism By Football

The Year Green Bay and the Packers Forged Their Futures

Tony Walter

M&B Global Solutions, Inc.
Green Bay, Wisconsin (USA)

Baptism By Football

The Year Green Bay and the Packers Forged Their Futures

First Edition

Disclaimer

The views expressed in this work are solely those of the author and do not necessarily reflect the views of the publisher, and the publisher hereby disclaims any responsibility for them. In the event you use any of the information in this book for yourself, which is your constitutional right, the author and the publisher assume no responsibility for your actions.

Front cover photos:
Curly Lambeau and the Hagemeister Park parking lot on a Green Bay Packers game day courtesy of the Neville Public Museum of Brown County

Back cover photo:
Author Tony Walter *(Jen Lucas Photography)*

ISBN 10: 1-942731-26-4
ISBN 13: 978-1-942731-26-9

Published by M&B Global Solutions Inc.
Green Bay, Wisconsin (USA)

Dedication

The greatest compliment that I ever receive is when I'm told I remind people of him. He wasn't in my life very long, but enough time to define honesty, fairness, love, and a Christian lifestyle that came with the expectation to pass it forward.

This book about Green Bay and the Packers is dedicated to my father, John Walter (1907-1959), and those whom I've been blessed to pass on his legacy: Jenny, Aran, Allison, John, Noah, Mark, Molly, Maxine, and Georgia.

Contents

Foreword

It was in the late 1970s when my wife and I traveled to Ireland, land of my ancestors. I was sports editor of the *Green Bay Press-Gazette*, with no little emphasis on the major sports interest of our readers: the Green Bay Packers.

We flew into Shannon Airport on the west side of Ireland, picked up our rental car, practiced driving on the opposite side of the street and headed directly to the city of Galway on the west coast. Our first stop was a typical Irish pub, where citizens – most of them men – were sitting on benches against the walls and drinking what I had to assume was Guinness.

Stepping to the bar as we soaked up the atmosphere, we saw it. Pinned to the wall behind the bar, in bold green and gold, was a huge Green Bay Packers pennant.

The story about pro football's most fascinating franchise wasn't confined to those who experienced it, grew up with it, wrote about it, or had visited the city whose identity embraced it.

Over the ensuing years, I read a lot about the Packers and was drawn to the years before I was born, before there was television, way before there was Internet. I heard a lot about it growing up because my father was a Green Bay native and had covered the Packers as sports editor of the *Press-Gazette* from 1935-41. In later years, I read more about the first eleven years of the Packers (1919-1929) and something started to catch my attention.

It seemed that every writer repeated much of the same information, not incorrectly but, to me, incompletely.

For example, the nickname given to five key men in the Packers' first decade – Curly Lambeau, Andrew Turnbull, Jerry Clifford, Dr. Webber Kelly, and Lee Joannes – by a Milwaukee sportswriter was the Hungry Five, an apparent reference to their ongoing campaign to keep the team financially afloat. No question, each of the men played a vital role in the franchise's growth and survival.

But I couldn't shake the sense that there had to be more to this unique story. There had to be more people, many more people, who had a hand in getting this sports phenomenon started and keeping it alive. Not only that, I believed it would be important to better understand what life was like, what issues had to be faced in Green Bay when pro football sought to wedge its way into the community fabric, long before it became the city's identity.

So, upon my retirement from the *Press-Gazette* after thirty-seven years in 2012, I decided to explore that period and find out. My principal source was the *Press-Gazette* itself, through microfilm at the Brown County Library and the Wisconsin State Historical Society in Madison. Other documents and books also helped unwrap this story. I intended to cover all ten years that preceded the Packers' first championship in 1929. I never got past 1922.

It was then, from January through December, that many major decisions were made that determined what Green Bay's citizens thought was important and determined what Green Bay would look like. In doing so, whether they knew it or not, they laid the foundation for the city's identity that remains today.

Of course, those days weren't like today's days in and around Green Bay. To fully understand how the Packers were born and nurtured, one needs to understand what else was going on, what obstacles and expectations were present in 1922. There was no Lambeau Field, no television, no marketing. There was no ticket-selling talent yet such as Johnny Blood or Don Hutson. There were just people who grabbed on to an entertainment they found enjoyable and wanted to help it be successful. And there were people who sought to improve the living and working conditions in Green Bay, to advance its reputation and impact its identity for future generations.

A world war had ended, women were finally allowed to vote, and their skirts were getting shorter. It was unlawful to make or sell alcohol. Automobiles were changing the country, there was anticipation that ocean ships would be coming to the Green Bay harbor soon, and there were people who were falling in love with a still-new entertainment industry, motion pictures.

The world knows of Green Bay and its football story. What follows is the story of the community in 1922 when there were no guarantees of future chapters, a time long before Green Bay separated itself from every other city and produced the blueprint for a one-of-kind epic sports story. Many of the names will be familiar, some for the legacies they left behind in terms of parks, streets, buildings and businesses that exist almost a century later. Relatives of some of the people still live in or around Green Bay.

The story is fascinating, especially for fans of history and those who have any stake or interest in Green Bay and its most famous property. You won't find another one like it.

Prologue

It's likely that Lawrence LaFond had never seen so much money in his life. He was just ten years old and living with his mother, Mary, on Main Street in Green Bay, in a building that housed five families just four blocks east of the Fox River.

Lawrence's father had died three years earlier in the flu epidemic that struck the area in 1918. His mother was trying to make a living as a machinist at the Green Bay Awning and Tent Company a block down the street.

So when banker Wilbur R. Whittenburg phoned Lawrence on that December day in 1921 to tell him he was the winner of $100, the boy was speechless. He had entered a contest sponsored by city retailers to come up with a slogan for Green Bay that business leaders hoped would both promote the community as a destination for a populace that fast was becoming mobile, and contribute to the city's quest to establish its own identity in the post-World War I generation.

Lawrence's slogan, "Gateway to the Great Waterway," seemed like the natural image to judges Whittenburg, Mayor Wenzel Wiesner, attorney Victor Minahan, and furniture executives Niels Ferslev and Edwin Krippner.

After all, connecting Green Bay's image to the Fox River, the bay of Green Bay, the Great Lakes, and the Atlantic Ocean was logical and timely, or so it seemed. Talks were ongoing between the United States and Canada to create the deep-channel St. Lawrence Seaway and open ports like Green Bay's to world commerce.

A report submitted a year earlier to the Green Bay City Council by renowned Harvard University urban planner John Nolen was still a hot topic. He was the same man who helped develop Madison's urban design (and has a major thoroughfare in that city named for him). In 1909, he prepared the design for Wisconsin's state park system that led to the development of Peninsula State Park in Door County, Devil's Lake State Park, Wyalusing State Park, and the protection of the Wisconsin River at Wisconsin Dells.

Retained by Green Bay in 1920, Nolen immediately saw the advantages of the river and bay on the city's portfolio. To him, it was obvious where the city should concentrate its attention in shaping its future. Nolen believed Green Bay's identity was about its location and what it promised for the future.

"Geographically, the city is so situated as to become a premier port and with that a great industrial and distribution center of the State of Wisconsin," he wrote. "Upon the realization of the Great Lakes-St. Lawrence deep waterway bringing ocean shipping to Green Bay docks much of the city's future depends.

"Upon the broad foundation herein laid down, it will be possible for the people of Green Bay to rear a city that will take its place as one of the most progressive communities of the United States, and opportunity is at hand, pointing the way for Green Bay to become a city with a reputation for convenience, order, well-being and all those qualities that make life in this world worth living."

But apparently, progressive thought wasn't at the forefront of Green Bay leadership's mindset in 1921. Optimism didn't translate into action.

Nolen's report, still stored in the basement of Green Bay City Hall, included two strong recommendations, one which took almost eighty years to be seriously acted upon and the other that was completely ignored. He urged city leaders to move its port businesses closer to the river's confluence with the bay and develop the Fox River frontage between the Walnut and Main Street bridges for public use and recreation – in other words, a parkway. And he proposed that the city develop a central square along Walnut Street between Jefferson and Adams streets, with green space and a bandstand to be bordered by municipal buildings. It never happened, despite Mayor Wiesner's vow to the Green Bay Rotary Club that Nolen's recommendations "would be the basis of action by the City Council as rapidly as its recommendations could be carried into effect."

The city's park superintendent, Marshall Simonds, endorsed Nolen's ideas of creating park space along the river and bay shores.

"With a good drive from the city out to the bay and a beautiful drive along the shore through the pleasant park surrounding, what city could boast of anything better?" Simonds said.

Green Bay, like so many other communities, was in search of its purpose and identity in the changing world of 1921. To what would the city attach its reputation and signature for the future?

John Kline
Editor of the
Green Bay Press-Gazette
(Photo courtesy Press-Gazette)

John Kline, editor of the *Green Bay Press-Gazette*, expressed the uncertainty that hung over the city.

"If we could come back to Green Bay, even 100 years hence, what would life be like?" Kline wrote in an editorial eighteen days before the end of 1921. "What would be the division of labor? Into what new fields would electricity have led us? What would be the achievements of science and invention? What would be the status of social and spiritual life? What would be the conditions of health? To what extent would the intricate economic methods of today be simplified or developed?

"It seems probable that future civilizations will have a system so complicated that the best auditors of 1921 could not grasp its workings. But it's not futile to attempt to discern the tendencies of modern life and to direct them along certain lines. Are we giving attention to fundamentals that we ought to give, or are we living in a haphazard age in which, while it cannot be said we are exactly drifting, we nevertheless cannot say with certainty and security along just what path we are traveling or to what end."

Question marks hovered over the city as 1921 came to a close.

The railroad industry, the largest employer in Green Bay, faced serious labor issues in a city that relied heavily on trains for the moving of passengers and freight. The National Prohibition Act of 1919, known informally as the Volstead Act, outlawed the production and sale of liquor. It was finding stubborn acceptance, if not open defiance, in Green Bay. The role of women was still being debated despite passage of the Nineteenth Amendment in 1920, which granted American women the right to vote. Only men were allowed to serve on juries in Brown County, and the Green Bay Police Department continued to resist the hiring of a female matron.

> *"It costs a lot of money to put a team like the Packers in the field. If we're going to continue to have this super grade of football, the ticket box receipts have got to show a big increase."*
>
> ***- Packers supporter Art Masse***

Infrastructure demanded attention, including highway and street paving, upgrade of city bridges, expansion of the streetcar routes, and improvement of city public school buildings. The city lacked sufficient modern hotel space, it had inadequate YMCA facilities, its museum was undefined, and its development of an accessible beach was incomplete.

There was plenty of industry in paper, cheese, pickles, and manufacturing. The former breweries were making soft drinks and candy, supposedly.

There was one other element – albeit fairly new and still without solid footing – striving to be one of the city's calling cards as 1921 ended.

It was professional football.

A team that had been thrown together more than two years earlier had represented itself well in competition with other state and

Midwestern city teams, and had found a place for itself in the new American Football League in 1921. Called the Packers, the team was led by Green Bay native Earl (Curly) Lambeau – as player, coach and ringleader – and was relying heavily on the unceasing print promotion from George W. Calhoun, sports editor of the *Press-Gazette.*

Their vision went beyond the neighborhood skirmishes, as Calhoun wrote during the 1921 season.

"The football situation has reached a showdown," he wrote, trying to drum up higher attendance at home games and get the organization out of the red. "Do the fans want to have the team keep on playing the Minneapolis Marines, Rock Island, Hammond and the elevens of the same class or do they want Oshkosh, Kaukauna, Sheboygan, Marinette and some of the other aggregations booked?"

Art Masse, an insurance agent who joined several other residents to form a booster club for the Packers, wrote about the necessity to get more fans at home games.

"It costs a lot of money to put a team like the Packers in the field," he wrote. "If we're going to continue to have this super grade of football, the ticket box receipts have got to show a big increase."

Finances weren't the only football issue facing a showdown. A cloud hung over the franchise as 1921 drew to an end. The team's survival was uncertain, its reputation as a play-fair organization was being called into question, its place in the league was in doubt, and its role in Green Bay's future legacy was still nothing more than a pipe dream.

Pro football in Green Bay – circa 1921 – fit Kline's definition of drifting through a haphazard age. He wrote in September 1921: "Football is one of the many sports that distinguishes Green Bay. We never invest anything in sports that does not yield large dividends."

The Packers' empire that exists in the twenty-first century has paid dividends, for sure. It will remain the centerpiece of the city's identity unless football is banned or someone in Green Bay invents a formula for world peace or immortality.

That's not how it was at the end of 1921.

Instead, Green Bay was like any other city of its size moving through a post-war, increasingly mobile but not fully modern world, eager to thrive and to believe it could become significant enough that others would take note. It provided a postcard of its time, of its past and its future.

As 1922 dawned, Green Bay had twenty-four barbershops and fifty-three dressmakers. It had twelve auto dealers but five blacksmith shops. There were sixteen cigar manufacturing shops and seven junk dealers, twenty-eight music teachers and nine billiard halls. There were twenty-seven hotels or boarding houses, four telegraph companies, six tinsmiths, and five undertakers.

There was one midwife. There were no malls.

But a cornerstone was about to be placed, leading to the development of several landmarks that remain today, reinforcing the city's determination to remain a community grounded in work, family, and pleasure, and to plant seeds that would give it a reputation beyond the reach of any other place in the land.

The year Nineteen Hundred Twenty-Two provided, more than any other year, the foundation for Green Bay's appearance for the next century and its identity for the present and future. This is how and when a small city started to become big in the world's eyes.

Chapter 1

January

Loss of a Franchise

The year started in relative serenity, with church bells ringing and factory whistles blowing as midnight arrived on that Saturday night. The general assumption was that most party-goers kept their alcoholic drink of choice well-concealed as they celebrated.

It was, after all, the age of Prohibition and a minimum of restraint was expected, even in a city where access to liquor never really abated. For the record, there were no arrests in Green Bay on New Year's Eve or New Year's Day 1922, which could also be a reflection of the regard that law enforcement had for the "dry" law.

The biggest party took place at the Elks Clubhouse at the corner of North Jefferson and Cherry streets, where more than 300 showed up on New Year's Day afternoon and some didn't leave until 5 a.m. the following day.

Green Bay's population was continuing to grow in the third decade of the twentieth century. There had been a 23 percent increase from 1910 to 1920 – the city's population was just over 31,000 as the year began – which enabled Green Bay to pass Oshkosh and Sheboygan and become the state's fourth-largest city. As a result, one of the issues

The Elks Club: The Green Bay Elks Clubhouse, built in 1901, was located on the northwest corner of North Jefferson Street and Cherry Street (now the site of Associated Bank's parking lot). It was there that hundreds gathered on New Year's Day 1922 despite Prohibition's "dry" law, and later would come to hear play-by-play of Packers road games that were sent by telegraph. The building was razed in 1962. *(Photo courtesy of the Neville Public Museum of Brown County)*

---

facing the city as 1922 began was the inadequate number of homes available.

The Belgian Flemish and the Danish had settled on the west side of the Fox River, leaving much of the east side to the Belgian Walloon and Polish, who arrived after the turn of the century. German, Irish and Scandinavian residents sprinkled throughout the city. These were the days before the number of Native Americans living in the city was even recorded.

The city, like the country, was still dealing with the effects of the business recession of 1920 and 1921. The return of troops after the World War meant a surge in the labor force. Wholesale prices dropped 36 percent in 1921, unemployment went from 5.2 percent to 11 percent, and the Federal Reserve Bank raised the interest rate from 4.75 percent to 7 percent. There was also a sharp drop in agricultural commodity prices.

City residents were told to expect a positive turn in the recession, and Kline all but promised it in a New Year's Eve editorial.

"Nineteen Twenty-two will be a year of prosperity," he wrote. "Business concerns of all kinds have wiped out their obligations and reorganized their affairs. Stocks are low. Money is plentiful, and it will seek channels of investment as soon as the final economic accommodations are attractive. Fundamental conditions warrant the firmest confidence that next year will be a prosperous one."

Economist H.C. Baldwin of the Babson Statistical Institute said three things were certain to occur in 1922. Production would exceed consuming capacity. There would be a sweeping readjustment of prices and wages. And there would be a great increase in industrial efficiency.

There was good news immediately after the New Year celebrations had ended. The Chicago, Milwaukee and St. Paul Railroad Co., with its depot on South Washington Street, announced it was calling 135 shopmen back to work in Green Bay, although some would only be able to work part-time for a while. These were among the 350 who were laid off three weeks earlier.

The expectation of reduced wages throughout the railroad industry cast a sense of dread throughout the country. Green Bay was no different.

Four railroad companies served the city: the Chicago & North Western; the Chicago, Milwaukee and St. Paul; the Green Bay & Western; and the Kewaunee, Green Bay & Western. No fewer than thirty-two trains arrived and departed from the city daily.

It was with anticipation that the city's Association of Commerce, predecessor to the Chamber of Commerce, welcomed officials from the Chicago, Milwaukee & St. Paul Railroad for a meeting to discuss possible expansion of service. Local businessmen wanted daily train service to and from Iron Mountain, Michigan, to improve their access to the Upper Peninsula (U.P.) customers.

The railroad sent two of its officials to Green Bay to talk about it. George R. Haynes was general passenger agent and E.G. Hayden was general agent of the passenger department. They said they would get train service to Iron Mountain by the spring. City officials said that wasn't soon enough. They countered by saying they wanted it immediately. They got it two months later.

This wasn't the only transportation issue that confronted the city at the start of the year. The city's streetcar system, operated by Wisconsin Public Service since 1894, was looking to expand. For six cents, residents could ride any of the six electric streetcar lines that dotted the community, reaching as far as Duck Creek on the northwest side and Kaukauna to the south.

The problem was the Main Street Bridge was the only city bridge that provided streetcar access across the Fox River, and the bridge was in very poor shape. A solution came when the City Council decided to spend $138,000 to add a streetcar line across the Walnut Street Bridge and continue as far west as Oneida Street. It was to be a temporary fix as the Walnut Street Bridge, built in 1863, would have to be replaced before long.

The city wasn't immune to human tragedy, and it appeared in many forms that month. Dorothy Kollman, a five-year-old who lived on South Chestnut Street died when her house burned. John Kocha, the thirty-seven-year-old father of five motherless children, was killed

Smoking, Swearing and Pool Playing

Rev. A.T. Erickson of the First Baptist Church outlined what he expected of men in the city.

"There are two varieties of men, those who seek and those who are sought. The seekers are the incompetent ones, the leaners, petitioners, and always have their hand out. They worship luck and strive for the short way to success.

"The men who are sought are those who encourage the weak, give wisdom to those in problems and have the strength to struggle with the causes. True courtesy is their hallmark.

"In dress, avoid singularity and slovenliness. Plucked eyebrows, manicured hands and perfume are as unmanly as rusty shoes, dirty ties and grease-spotted clothes. Some of the young man's habits to avoid are tobacco. It is a drug to which the system is not accustomed and is a rank negative poison. Drink I need not mention. It is gone and its evils are already acknowledged."

as he worked in a railroad car shop. A rivet flew off and punctured his windpipe and jugular vein. Mary Lou Van Boxel, the mother of three daughters, was diagnosed with typhoid.

Health was, of course, a constant concern, especially after the deadly flu crisis that had killed hundreds in the community a few years earlier. The city was functioning with three hospitals, all on the east side and in close proximity to each other.

The largest was St. Vincent with its 300 beds on South Webster Avenue. A few blocks to the north, St. Mary's Hospital provided 150 beds, and between those two institutions was the smaller Deaconess Hospital with its sixty beds, although there were already plans to expand it under the guidance of Dr. Julius Bellin.

Internationally, the Irish were trying, unsuccessfully, to agree on a peace plan that would give them self-rule from England. The world's Roman Catholic community prepared to elect a new pope when Pope Benedict XV died.

For drama in the Brown County court system, local resident Katie Jurgykowski sued Anton Klarkowski for $5,000, claiming he didn't keep his promise to marry her. She was awarded $125. And Judge Henry Graass granted an annulment to Francis Fortin after Fortin discovered that the French woman he married in Paris in 1919 didn't actually have two brothers, but two sons, and the chances were good that her first husband was still alive.

This was a pivotal time for the Green Bay Packers. The organization was being investigated by the American Football League after a sportswriter for a Chicago newspaper accused the Packers of illegally using amateur college players in a game. Many Green Bay people concluded that Chicago Bears player-coach George Halas was the source of the report, although it was never confirmed.

The Packers never really denied the charge, the only semblance of a defense being their claim that most of the pro teams used college athletes playing under assumed names, a claim that league president Joseph E. Carr believed, but had yet to act upon in his first year leading the league. The game in question was the December 4, 1921, game in Milwaukee against Racine. Three Notre Dame football players – Heatley Anderson, Fred Larson and Arthur Garvey – played in the game and were subsequently banished from all future Notre Dame sports teams.

Anderson, in his 1976 autobiography, claimed he played against the Packers in that game, but most evidence indicates he played for Lambeau, himself a former Notre Dame football player and ex-teammate of Anderson's. Anderson went on to play and coach for the Chicago Bears, so it's possible he didn't want his name associated with the Bears' top rival.

The confrontation between college and pro football was reaching a crescendo. The pro game's biggest critics were Notre Dame football coach Knute Rockne and University of Chicago coach Amos Alonzo Stagg, for obvious reasons.

Rockne went on the offensive.

"Professionalism is the menace to college football," he said. "Unless the tendency in that direction is curtailed, it may be necessary to abolish the game as an intercollegiate sport. Football has taken a wonderful hold on the public in the last ten years. If its popularity is to continue, professionalism and the gambler must be terminated."

Calhoun rebutted in print.

"If we remember correctly, it wasn't so many years ago that Rock picked up some sideline cash by playing with the teams in Ohio. He probably has had a direct change of heart since the happenings of this past fall."

But Calhoun did write that he agreed with Rockne's comment that football is a cure for the effeminate male, whom he called "cake-eaters."

Stagg organized a campaign against the use of college players by the pros.

"It is time that we stopped it," he said.

Calhoun seemed to be trying to convince himself that nothing would come of the matter, writing "We have a hunch that the alleged scandal will blow over without any fireworks."

He argued that any sins of the Packers were shared by the other pro teams.

"It is a well-known fact that nearly all of the pro squads make use

A Movie Landmark

What turned out to be the biggest movie of the year, The Sheik, began a long run at the Strand Theater. It starred new sensation Rudolph Valentino and Agnes Ayres, and was about a man who followed the maxim that "When an Arab sees a woman he wants, he takes her."

The show was available at normal Strand Theater prices, although it played to advanced prices in Milwaukee and other cities.

of the college players while they are still members of varsity teams. In these days of frenzied finances, a hundred bucks or so a game looks pretty good to the youth in college and many are willing to take a chance of pulling through without getting caught," Calhoun wrote. "Right off the bat, we could name a half dozen Western Conference stars, supposed to be in good amateur standing, who in the last year or two have piled up jack now and then mixing with the professional athletes under assumed names. We don't defend the action ... but we can't help but wonder how it is going to be stopped."

Calhoun defended the Packers against a story in a Chicago newspaper that implied a December 1921 game between the Packers and a Chicago-area team called Morse Supreme was cancelled because fans in the Windy City were upset about the Green Bay team's use of college players.

"We have to laugh at the folly of the statement," Calhoun wrote. "It is about as near right as any of those Chicago sports scribes ever get anything. The game was called off because the Morse Supreme team wouldn't meet the guarantee."

Nevertheless, the league was under pressure to stop the pro teams' use of amateur players. A meeting of team owners was set for the last week of the month in Canton, Ohio, and the rumors were floating that something might have to change in Green Bay.

In fact, it already was changing. The Clair brothers – John and Emmett – who were granted the Packers franchise by the new American Association of Professional Football at a meeting at Chicago's LaSalle Hotel in August 1921, were already separating themselves from Green Bay. John Clair was secretary of the Indian Packing Company when it sponsored the Packers in 1919. He was made vice president a year later when it was purchased by the Chicago-based Acme Packing Company.

Vitamin Discovery

Elmer McCollum and a team of scientists at Johns Hopkins University discover vitamin D, a substance they found in cod liver oil that prevents rickets. It would eventually lead to the development of vitamin-fortified milk.

But the Clair brothers severed their ties with the Acme plant in Green Bay and moved to Chicago. Rumors persisted that they wanted to transfer the Packers franchise to Chicago with them, but it was just one of many rumors swirling around the football team at the time.

When the league owners met in Canton late in the month, the timing couldn't have been worse for the Packers.

The day before the meeting opened, the University of Illinois announced it was suspending nine football players permanently. This went back to a 1920 scandal in which two small Illinois cities – Carlinville and Taylorville – made ample use of college players in a football game in which $50,000 changed hands through the betting in both communities. Eventually, Notre Dame also suspended several players who played in the game, including Joey Sternamann, who went on to play for the Chicago Bears.

In a 1983 interview, Sternamann denied that college players painted their faces to hide their identities in the game.

"Everybody at the game knew who we were," he said.

Emmett Clair showed up at the owners meeting, and after discussing the Packers case, made a motion to have the Packers franchise surrendered. The owners passed it unanimously. All Carr would tell Green Bay officials was that some decision about a new Packers franchise would be made by June 1.

Carr did release a statement that he probably knew wasn't completely true.

"Our association was formed, mainly, for the purpose of stamping out the practice of professional football teams signing college players before they have completed their college career. Our rules are very definite on this matter. The only member of the association to break this rule this fall was the Green Bay Packers. The team was dropped from the association by unanimous vote of directors of the association."

Back in Green Bay, Lambeau began meeting with some businessmen in an effort to reorganize with a new leadership team, but the month ended with the Packers on the outside of pro football and looking in.

"Capt. Lambeau has been conversing with businessmen here and they are unanimous in their opinion that Green Bay should be represented in the league, if not by the Packers, then some other team," Calhoun wrote.

One last official order of business in the month: the City Council passed an ordinance declaring that ashes could no longer be dumped on the streets.

Chapter 2

February

Religion and a Snow Job

Green Bay was a predominantly Catholic community, so news and issues that affected the faith had an impact. One week into the month, Cardinal Ratti was elected the new pontiff and became Pope Pius XI.

Many of the city's churches were located in neighborhoods dominated by specific ethnic groups. The Germans frequented St. Francis Xavier Cathedral, the Dutch at St. Willebrord, the Irish at St. Patrick, the Polish at St. Mary's of the Angels, and the Belgians at SS. Peter and Paul.

At the same time, a war of words was taking place between a nationally known politician and a state educator. William Jennings Bryan, a former presidential candidate who a few years later would take the literal Bible side against the theory of evolution in the famous Scopes trial, accused University of Wisconsin President Edward A. Birge of being an atheist because he accepted many of the conclusions of modern science.

Female Jurist Takes Charge

Mrs W.H. Simpler of Green Bay became the first female jury member in Brown County and was chosen jury foreman in her first trial. It involved Clemenz Freitman, who sued the Green Bay Sugar Company after some of his furniture was damaged by company officials when they transported them to his home. The company was found negligent and careless, and Freitman was awarded $89.50 by the jury.

Birge fired back.

"I've never found it necessary to justify religion to science or excuse science to religion," he said. "I have accepted both as divine revelations and both as equally wrought into the constitution of the world. I have believed that wisdom and might are God's and I have equally believed that science reveals to us how that might and wisdom are expressed in the operation of the world."

A skirmish developed after the publication of a story that indicated the directors of the National Federation of Club Women, meeting in Chautauqua, New York, passed a resolution favoring birth control.

Immediately, Mrs. John F. Martin, a member of the Catholic Women of Green Bay, responded, noting that the local club was associated with the national federation.

"No Catholic woman is allowed to belong to an organization which advocates doctrines contrary to the teaching of the Church, for by this act of membership do they contribute to the running expenses of pernicious propaganda."

Mrs. Francis T. Blesch of Green Bay attended a meeting of the national federation and got to the bottom of the matter.

In a telegram to friends in Green Bay, she wired, "Please say to the Press-Gazette that the report was false. The General Federation of Women's Clubs has not endorsed birth control and the New York Federation that did endorse it has rescinded its action. We think that some reporters who were not allowed in the executive session did this for spite."

No record could be found to show how this debate played out in the Green Bay pulpits, but it is certain morality concerns were common themes. A University of Missouri official, visiting the area, sounded the alarm.

"We have come upon a reign of moral looseness and debauchery," said Dr. Jay William Hudson. "Students dance as people were not allowed to dance in the worst resorts 20 years ago. There is a heathenistic trend."

Annie Laurie, an advice columnist, reacted strongly when two eighteen-year-old women asked the best way to meet two boys they had seen at a "moving picture place."

Wrote Laurie: "You are doing a very indiscreet and possibly dangerous thing, girls, by flirting with young men. There is no way to meet them without being introduced to them by mutual friends."

And County Judge Henry Graass said, "We must take boys away from streets and pool halls."

There were nine billiard halls in the city and plenty of streets.

Religion was a major cornerstone to the Green Bay lifestyle, but the bridge between the Protestant and Catholic denominations showed little signs of shortening.

Wrote Kline: "Nothing is so dangerous as religious prejudice, which almost inevitably tends to fanaticism."

> *"People trip the light fantastic with their cheeks pressed close together and their bodies as close as will permit. It is terrible.*
>
> ***- Charles Bayard Mitchell***
> *Bishop in the*
> *Methodist Episcopal Church*

The previous year, Charles Bayard Mitchell, a bishop in the Methodist Episcopal Church, had lamented that morals had fallen to great depths.

"People trip the light fantastic with their cheeks pressed close together and their bodies as close as will permit. It is terrible," he said.

The Dean of Women at the University of Wisconsin weighed in, too. "Cheek-to-cheek demonstrations are only cheap vulgarisms," she said, blaming the growing popularity of the saxophone and clarinet.

It was also the time of the flapper craze, where women wore their skirts a little shorter, their hair bobbed, and their footwear with flat heels. Gasp!

News that would have a major impact on the community's future

Paper Becomes Big Business: A crew poses with a paper machine in the Hoberg Paper Company's mill on the northeast side of Green Bay. The company later became known as the Charmin Paper Company and later would be purchased by Procter & Gamble. *(Photo courtesy of Neville Public Museum of Brown County)*

---

occurred on the first day of the month. The Hoberg Paper Company merged with Green Bay Fibre and Paper Company to become Hoberg Paper & Fibre, reducing the area's number of paper companies from four to three. John Hoberg had opened his paper mill in 1895 after working for Kimberly-Clark.

The 1922 merger came two years before Hoberg spent $250,000 to build an addition to its paper plant and six years before the company introduced its signature product – Charmin tissue – and twenty-eight years before it changed its name to Charmin Paper Company. Later, it was purchased by Procter & Gamble.

Paper production was fast becoming the major industry in the Green Bay area, due in large part to the access to water and the abundance of lumber. Northern Paper Mills, at the junction of the Fox and East rivers, was the largest paper mill in the city – over 600 employees – and already billed itself as the top manufacturer of tissue in the world. It remained under that title until being purchased by James River in 1982 and is now part of Georgia-Pacific.

The newest entry in the paper production business was the Fort Howard Paper Company at the border of Green Bay and Ashwaubenon. It was started just three years earlier by Prussia native Austin E. Cofrin, a former plant superintendent for Northern Paper. Fort Howard was in the throes of expansion by its third year of production and planned a new three-story building.

For sure, Green Bay was a major player in the country's paper producing industry. Association of Commerce Managing Director William F. Kerwin said the three mills had the capacity to produce 200 tons of tissue daily; that one day's work could make enough paper strips four-and-a-half inches wide to wrap around the world twice.

James H. McGillan
Green Bay city booster
(Photo courtesy of Neville Public Museum of Brown County)

It was an industry that wasn't immune to the financial stresses of the day. Employees of the Northern Paper Mills, Hoberg and Green Bay Fibre and Paper companies staged strikes in 1921 to protest reduced wages. The companies survived the work stoppages.

The city was in the midst of getting itself organized. An ordinance was passed to create five zones – residential, first business, second business, industrial, and unrestricted, which Mayor Wiesner said, "In from one to five generations will mark Green Bay as a pioneer in the now almost untouched field of orderly, efficient, carefully planned civic development."

The push was also on to promote the city. A contest was held to choose an official Green Bay song, and Annie Robinson, who lived on East Mason Street, won. Her lyrics included "The gateway to lake and ocean, Green Bay stands for fortune and fame."

James H. McGillan keynoted a meeting of city boosters at the

Snowbound: These residents along Velp Avenue managed to maneuver through the huge snowbanks that buried the city in February 1922. Some weather officials said it was the biggest snowstorm in memory and stopped rail and auto traffic for days. *(Photo courtesy of Neville Public Museum of Brown County)*

Strand Theater on South Washington Street by puffing up the city's image.

"Green Bay is a clean city, physically and morally, and we ought to be glad to let it be known. It is so known outside, so why wouldn't we raise our voices in praise of our city?"

It's doubtful that promoters used the weather as poster material. The month included one of the heaviest winter storms in memory, with sleet and snow falling for forty straight hours, piling drifts six feet high. All trains halted and many wires were down. Emmett Platten, a west side butcher, used his amateur radio to keep community leaders apprised of the storm. Alf C. Witteborg, owner of the Beaumont Hotel, held a dance for stranded businessmen and, we can assume, some women.

F.W. Conrad, chief of the Green Bay weather bureau, said it was the biggest storm he experienced in his more than thirty years at the bureau. He said 3.42 inches of precipitation fell during the storm, but the total snowfall couldn't be measured because the snow gauge located on the roof of the Minahan Building became ice-covered and had to be removed.

The last train to leave Green Bay before the tracks became impassable was a Chicago & North Western passenger train that left twenty-four hours after the storm began. But it derailed near Little Chute, with an engineer and fireman injured.

William Ronning, a Wisconsin Telephone Company employee, was at the Little Chute depot at the time of the derailment. He reported the incident to Green Bay officials after traveling to the city the following day ... by foot.

It took more than 200 men with shovels to eventually clear streets and intersections, and trains were running on schedule three days after the storm ended. The storm was estimated to have caused more than $500,000 damage, with no mail coming or leaving the city for two days and only one telephone circuit, to Shawano, open during most of the storm.

This didn't stop Lambeau, then serving as East High School athletic director, from taking a group of boys on a fifteen-mile ski hike to Lily Lake in eastern Brown County. Among the participants were Tom Hearden, Austin Straubel, William Servotte and Donald Irmiger.

The area saw two progressive steps taken. The Brown County Museum, which was housed in the basement of the county library on South Jefferson Street, incorporated. This was the work of Arthur Neville and Deborah Martin, whose footprints on area history would become permanent.

And the Green Bay Police Department finally broke the gender line. Ida Graves of Waupun was hired to be the department's first female matron at a salary of $100 a month.

Matron Goes to Work

Ida Graves, the first female matron for the Green Bay Police Department, submitted her first monthly report, indicating she was involved with more than twenty cases involving young girls. She sent four of them to their homes in other cities and found positions for five others in county homes. The majority of the cases involved girls between the ages of fourteen and sixteen.

Dr. Julius Bellin announced he was adding two floors to the Bellin Building at the corner of Washington and Walnut streets. There was speculation he wanted his building to be taller than the six-story Minahan Building constructed seven years earlier by Dr. J. R. Minahan, whose allegiance was to St. Vincent Hospital.

> **_New Magazine_**
>
> DeWitt and Lila Wallace introduced their new weekly magazine, calling it *The Reader's Digest.*

The professional football issue continued to fester, although the Packers remained outside the pro league. A *Press-Gazette* editorial claimed that "professionalism in athletic sports has corrupted college athletic teams. Professionalism has always been a menace to the power of good that exists in the form of amateur athletics. It is more of a menace now that it has ever been before."

But Calhoun maintained his forum and raised some interesting points.

"The college rule against professionalism is not fair in some cases," wrote the *Press-Gazette's* sports editor. He wanted to know why college swimmers could still get jobs as paid lifeguards, or why members of a college debate team would receive compensation for participating in debate tours, which were popular then.

"But let the football, basketball or baseball player get in the dollar class and he is immediately blacklisted, if caught."

As the month ended, the Packers were still dealing with the fact they were caught.

College coaches began discussions about changing the football rules. Their biggest concern was their perception that the forward pass was getting out of control. One proposal suggested that an incomplete pass should result in the ball being placed from the spot the pass was thrown and not at the original line of scrimmage. It didn't get much support.

Chapter 3

March

Prohibition ... Kind of Maybe

Old-timers liked to repeat a comment that was attributed to former President Ulysses S. Grant when he came to Green Bay in 1880 to visit a friend, Sen. Timothy O. Howe. Walking along Main Street and noticing no shortage of saloons, Grant supposedly said, "Well, I don't see any need of any of you Green Bay folks going thirsty."

Green Bay's affection for intoxicating liquor was no secret. But it occasionally led to trouble.

William Eugene "Pussyfoot" Johnson was a nationally known Prohibition advocate and former law enforcement officer who traveled the country speaking out against booze. Immediately prior to his speech at the Union Congregational Church on South Madison Street, a bomb exploded. It must not have been much of a bomb, because none of the 500 people in attendance was injured. It made a loud noise and Frank Walker of Green Bay picked it up and threw it outside. Someone, obviously, had strong feelings about Prohibition, but no one was apprehended.

Typhoid Scare

A threat of typhoid fever brought the Green Bay water system under attack. Twenty employees of the John Hoberg Paper Company sought compensation for disabilities due to typhoid fever they claimed was the result of drinking water from the company's well.

Aetna, the insurance company representing Hoberg, claimed the bad water came from a leak in the city's water pipes after East River water seeped into the city pipes that ran along the bottom of the East River near Jackson Street. Insurance investigators insisted the city pipes were damaged by pilings that left it susceptible to dirty river water.

City water was being funneled to businesses and residents from deep artesian wells. The State Board of Health held hearings to investigate the matter, first instructing Hoberg to disconnect water from his well. F.E. Church, a bacteriologist for the Milwaukee Health Department, testified at the Milwaukee hearing on the issue. He noted that of the thirty-five random samplings of Green Bay's water system, thirty-two showed bacterial results sufficient to indicate the water wasn't safe. But Ferdinand Krueger, a Milwaukee Water Plant engineer, said there was no chance that river water got into the city water supply.

The Wisconsin Industrial Commission ruled in favor of the plant employees and awarded a total of $3,976.

Kline, in an editorial, wrote that it really didn't matter which side was right.

"It doesn't matter whether the water itself is pure this particular moment or not. The fact remains that it is liable to be contaminated at any time. The methods of storing water are obsolete and dangerous. The use of an open well is unsanitary."

Getting water from Lake Michigan was just a future dream and didn't become operational for another thirty-five years.

Liquor raids were common. Although fifty-nine saloons in the city closed after the Eighteenth Amendment was passed, many remained open and often paid a price for dealing in the liquor trade. A year earlier, saloon keeper William McGinnis was charged with selling eighty-seven gallons of whiskey and purchasing more than 1,000 gallons. He was eventually sentenced to five and a half months in jail and fined $2,500.

Roy Cox and James Mortell tried to be creative and camouflaged their still in a tent. But they were caught and fined.

No longer called saloons or taverns, these businesses were advertised as soft drink establishments. There were ninety of them in Green Bay in 1922, more than a third of them on Main Street. One of the biggest federal raids in the area occurred at the Entertainer Inn in Duck Creek, just northwest of Green Bay. Led by federal agent Thomas Martin of Green Bay, the raid confiscated 1,000 pint bottles of whiskey and 1,200 bottles of gin.

Enforcement of the non-liquor law was costly for Green Bay resident Thomas Delaney, who was the federal Prohibition director for Wisconsin. He was brought up on two charges of conspiracy to violate the Volstead Act and went to trial in Milwaukee. He was accused of taking bribes from Milwaukee wholesale liquor dealer Joseph Dudenhoefer, found guilty, and was sentenced to two years in prison and fined $10,000.

One federal agent testified to the grand jury in Milwaukee that Green Bay was "one of the wettest spots in the state." He said several automobiles with whiskey and colored alcohol had been seized recently en route to Green Bay.

Brown County District Attorney Carl Young went to the County Board and asked for $3,000 to hire an investigator to confront the county liquor traffic issue. He said the problem had reached almost alarming proportions in the county.

"For the past six months our office has received many complaints from practically every part of the county concerning the traffic of moonshine," Young wrote in his letter to supervisors. "Even young boys and girls are being promiscuously supplied with this kind of liquor. This office, under the circumstances, is wholly powerless. The moonshine situation in this county has become so serious and dangerous that some definite effective work should be done."

He didn't get the help.

What he got was verbiage instead. The Board voted in favor of Supervisor John Greenwood's resolution that urged Congress to get rid of Prohibition.

"The Volstead Act is daily causing dissatisfaction with and disrespect for so-called federal prohibition laws and tends to create disrespect for other laws and is generally condemned in all sections of our county by all classes of people," Greenwood's resolution read. "It's a notorious fact that the evils from the so-called moonshine traffic and manufacture of other intoxicating drinks in the private homes far outweigh the promised benefits."

Congress was unmoved.

At least one Green Bay brewery found itself in trouble, too. Rahr Brewery was ordered to close after being accused of manufacturing near beer. The brewery was fined $15,000 and owner Fred Rahr drew an eight-month sentence in a house of corrections. The brewery didn't stay closed for long.

Several tavern operators were also fined for making or selling liquor. The normal fine was $200, and most paid it and returned to business as usual.

Some help for the "dry" backers came from the Wisconsin Supreme Court, which ruled that home brew for the owner's consumption was illegal.

Green Bay's general disregard for the liquor law came with a touch of irony. The city had been the cradle of the state's temperance movement dating back to 1835, when 152 women formed the first Temperance Society. The women were disturbed at the easy access to alcohol soldiers had under Gen. Winfield Scott, commander at Fort Howard (located on the west bank of the Fox River).

But the city no longer led the charge by 1922. The Woman's Christian Temperance Union in Wisconsin began holding its annual conventions in 1874 and for the next half-century met in Milwaukee, Fond du Lac, Janesville, Waupun, Racine, Madison, Eau Claire, Sparta, Waukesha, Neenah, Baraboo, Oshkosh, La Crosse, Portage, Beloit, Appleton, Chippewa Falls, Wausau, Reedsburg, Antigo, Rhinelander, Ashland, Waupaca, or Superior.

Never in Green Bay, despite the fact the city was home to a dry enforcement office.

It wasn't just the violation of federal law that concerned officials in 1922. There was a health issue that emerged as more residents began making their own moonshine. One Green Bay resident, found dead in the East River, was deemed to have died from bad homemade liquor.

Judge Nicolas Monahan told one moonshiner, "You should be

Bridge problems: The old Main Street Bridge was in dilapidated condition when authorities closed it in 1921. Voters approved bonding for a new bridge in March 1922. Today's Titletown Brewing Company is visible across the river at left. *(Photo courtesy of Neville Public Museum of Brown County)*

---

sentenced to drink your own stuff."

Kline opined in the *Press-Gazette*, falling short of an endorsement of Prohibition but acknowledging it was the law of the land.

"It is hoped that this campaign will be more successful than efforts made thus far to rid America of the shameful conditions now making a mockery of the Prohibition law. If a majority of the people really are opposed to the Volstead Act, it should be modified by orderly process. So long as it stands on the statute books, defiance of it ought not to be tolerated."

In another editorial, Kline acknowledged that "liquor flows in and around Green Bay like water. Enforcement of the Volstead Act is a farce."

Green Bay and the rest of the country endured Prohibition for another eleven years before Congress finally passed the Twenty-first Amendment in 1933, shortly after Franklin D. Roosevelt was inaugurated. The amendment needed ratification by three-fourths of the states to become law, and it achieved that before the end of the year.

Michigan was the first state to ratify. Wisconsin was second on April 25, 1933.

One national movement that drew very little support in the Green Bay area and most of the rest of Wisconsin was the introduction of daylight saving time. It had been approved by Congress in 1918, but didn't get traction in the Green Bay area.

Rise of the streetcar: Workers install streetcar tracks on East Walnut Street. The tracks were active until the late 1930s. Soon after they were dug up and the metal used in the war effort. *(Photo courtesy of Neville Public Museum of Brown County)*

A resolution brought to the County Board said the idea "does not operate satisfactorily for the majority of the people and causes great inconvenience, loss and trouble to a large part of our population, and great confusion results."

The city and state remained opposed to the concept of daylight saving time for thirty-five more years. It was imposed by the U.S. Government in 1942 as War Time, but that was repealed when the war ended in 1945. A statewide referendum to adopt daylight saving time was approved in 1957 with 54.63 percent of the voters in support.

Voters went to the polls mid-month to decide if they favored $525,000 bonding to proceed with construction of a new Main Street Bridge. It was decisive, with bonding being approved 1,756-383.

But the path to building a new bridge wasn't a smooth one. Just a year earlier, public sentiment favored a concrete bridge instead of a steel bridge. The City Council voted for a steel bridge and hired the Strauss Bascule Bridge Company of Chicago to design it. That led to claims of favoritism when it was disclosed that City Engineer W.W. Reed, who had previously worked for Strauss, recommended his former employer a week before the public meeting was held to discuss options.

Reed wasn't shy about his defense of Joseph Strauss.

"His little finger contains more knowledge about building bridges than all the other engineers combined," he said.

Time was of the essence. The existing Main Street Bridge was closed to vehicle traffic in September 1921 because it was deemed unsafe. This created a logjam on the other two city bridges because the Main Street span was used more than either the Walnut Street or Mason Street bridges.

Eventually, Green Construction of Green Bay won the bid to build the bridge for $475,045. Strauss would go on to design the Lewis and Clark Bridge over the Columbia River in 1930 and served as chief engineer of the Golden Gate Bridge in San Francisco from 1933-37.

The debate continued locally and in Congress over funding for the Green Bay harbor channel, which needed to be deeper to allow lake ships to continue to come and go. The National Rivers and Harbor Congress, meeting in Washington, D.C., passed a resolution in support of making Green Bay's case a priority.

Congress appropriated $91,000 for the Green Bay harbor and $100,000 for the Fox River, amounts that were welcome in the city but were less than harbor officials wanted.

It all focused on what most assumed was the imminent approval of financing and construction of the St. Lawrence Seaway, a canal that would link the Great Lakes with the Atlantic Ocean and, thus, worldwide shipping to and from the Midwest.

The Wisconsin Bankers Association, with Green Bay's John Rose and Joseph Conway in attendance, passed a resolution urging Congress to get the project completed as soon as possible. The agricultural interests in Northeastern Wisconsin were eager to find outlets for their products beyond their current reach.

Just three years earlier, a large vessel loaded with anthracite coal couldn't get into the Green Bay ports because of the lack of channel depth. The coal went elsewhere. Many saw the port's future as the key to the city's future. A statement from Citizens National Bank was printed in the *Press-Gazette*.

"Although Green Bay has been a lake port of importance for

nearly 300 years, no city on the Great Lakes will receive greater impetus from the completion of the Great Lakes-St. Lawrence ship canal. Green Bay is looking ahead intelligently and is indeed the City Prepared."

Kline agreed.

"Without it we would be an ordinary second or third rate city all our lives," he wrote. "It is water and location that are to make Green Bay. It is water and location that today focuses attention on Wisconsin. Yet Green Bay has been woefully neglected in the improvement of its harbor. Green Bay has the most desirable location for the case of water transportation of any port on Lake Michigan. It is a vastly better port than Milwaukee. Within five years, the 4,000 miles of Great Lakes shoreline may be added to our sea coast. Within that time, vessels from Liverpool, Hamburg and the Havre may be sailing into Lake Michigan.

"The ship canal is going through, without any question."

Gandhi Arrested

Mohandas Gandhi was arrested and tried for sedition by British authorities in India. Found guilty, he was sentenced to six years in prison. Ghandi preached a non-violent protest and peaceful resistance to British rule.

Despite the optimism in Green Bay about ocean traffic making its way to its port through the St. Lawrence River and Great Lakes, the project wouldn't be completed until 1959, in no small part because of objections from the State of New York that didn't want its Erie Canal to become less traveled and eastern businesses to become less profitable.

Another issue that continued to fester involved street signs in Green Bay. There really weren't any that were up to date and visible. The Kiwanis and Rotary clubs decided to undertake the project as it was agreed the absence of updated markers presented a serious handicap for residents and visitors alike.

The Hartman-Greiling Co., located on the west riverfront, manufactured boats for the navy in World War I. It was succeeded by Northwest Engineering Co., which incorporated in 1921 and began producing industrial cranes that helped revolutionize the construction industry.

The Packers stayed out of the news, with its leaders waiting for June and a chance for forgiveness.

Chapter 4

April

Marketing Green Bay to the World

The community's image was a concern for many city leaders, and many of them spoke out about it.

A City Beautification Contest was held to generate ideas that would improve the city's appearance. Many entries focused on a need for homeowners to clean up their yards, but the top two awards went to residents who liked Nolen's proposals.

Paul Halloin won the top prize, suggesting that the city "teach every citizen what to do. Herald continuously from the pulpit, and press plans made by Mr. Nolen. Teach them in the schools." He urged the removal of smoke from industrial plants and a cleanup of the riverfront "because it shouldn't be hideous and shabby."

Deborah Martin, a librarian at the Kellogg Library, won second prize, urging the city to "carry out promptly John Nolen's plan for city improvement."

River traffic: The Fox River was a major thoroughfare for shipping traffic as the Port of Green Bay pushed to become a player on a global scale. Here, the tug *Cockamong* approaches the Main Street Bridge. *(Photo courtesy of Neville Public Museum of Brown County)*

Abbie Robinson wrote the prize-winning booster song for the city to tune of *Columbia, the Gem of the Ocean*:

"The gateway to lake and ocean
Green Bay stands for fortune and fame
True prophets of faith and devotion,
Wisconsin's first pioneers came
With the blessing of nature around her,
With man's courage and zeal holding sway,
May Prosperity ever surround her,
Three cheers for our ancient Green Bay.
Three cheers for our ancient Green Bay,
The gate to the great waterway.
May prosperity ever surround her,
Three cheers for our ancient Green Bay.

The judges who chose Robinson's song as the winner changed the word "ancient" to "glorious."

Kline took the lead in promoting the city and region in print.

"We who live in the Fox River Valley are missing a rare opportunity to capitalize on the wonderful advantages which we enjoy," wrote Kline in an editorial. "Most of us are going along on our tranquil, unseeing way, failing to realize that we possess resources in this wonderful valley of ours to enhance our wealth many fold if the rest of the world knew we had them. We have marvelous commercial and manufacturing possibilities, splendid agricultural land, fine educational institutions, excellent living conditions, everything that is desirable in making a home and a living. We cannot capitalize on these advantages unless other people know they are here."

> *"We who live in the Fox River Valley are missing a rare opportunity to capitalize on the wonderful advantages which we enjoy."*
>
> ***- Press-Gazette editor John Kline***

It prompted the Rotary, Kiwanis, Lions and civic business organizations to plan a study, hoping to get $50,000 from each of the four counties near Green Bay.

Circumstances favoring tourism in the Green Bay area were working in the city's favor. Tourist camps were established at both Bay Beach and Joannes Park to provide overnight destinations for travelers. Also, retail opportunities along Main Street were growing since the important state highways reaching Green Bay at the time were routed over Main Street.

The Brown County Board of Supervisors approved a $3,000 proposal to hire three or four motorcycle officers to patrol county roads outside Green Bay. But they really were intended to be "traveling information bureaus" to help visitors find their way around the area. Supervisors warned that the move "doesn't mean the bars will be let down and excessive speed countenanced."

A civic dinner was held to promote Green Bay as a destination. Among the speakers was Mrs. George Nau.

"This should be a red letter day in Green Bay," she said, "for it is the first time that we women have been invited to participate in any civic affairs, and we are very much pleased."

The Association of Commerce bragged that many industrial concerns were expressing interest in relocating to Green Bay because of the city's location and availability of factory sites. It sponsored a drive to recruit more association members and was surprised that its first four volunteers were women: Nathalie C. Green, Mrs. George D. Nau, Mrs. William J. Fisk, and Mrs Flora C. Clisby.

"The action of these Green Bay women surpasses anything in my experience," said Association President Dan Weigle. "I have never seen women anywhere display the enthusiasm that these women have shown."

A *Press-Gazette* editorial hailed the efforts to promote civic pride.

"A united city will make a greater Green Bay," it read. "The Green Bay Boosters have decided to establish a spirit in the campaign and from now on the question 'What can I put into Green Bay' will supersede the idea of 'What can I get out of it?'

"Picture to yourself Green Bay with over 30,000 people trying to put something in for a while instead of playing grab bag and everybody taking something out. Would Green Bay prosper? If Green Bay prospers, we all individually get our share. Forget self for a while and by the use of enlightened selflessness adopt the plan of wisdom and build a great city worthy to be the Gateway to the Great Waterway."

But Green Bay missed its chance to take advantage of John Nolen's recommendation. The city's port business remained near downtown and not closer to the confluence with the bay, and his idea of creating a city square between Jefferson and Adams streets never materialized. It wasn't until the end of the century that the city transformed the riverfront into a tourist-friendly site.

Nolen completed urban development projects throughout the country, most notably in San Diego, California, and Savannah, Georgia. He was elected president of the National Conference on City Planning in 1927 and died in 1937 at the age of sixty-eight.

Again, weather wasn't a friendly calling card in April. It rained each of the first twelve days of the month except two, causing flooding in some areas. Some railroad tracks were under water for days and trains had to take detour routes. It caused sewer backups as well.

Albert Maes offered some humor. He brought two small fish to the mayor's office that he said he found swimming down Howard Street in flooded waters. Named Jack and Jill, the fish were placed in an aquarium.

There were some impressive statistics in the business world. The nine banks in Green Bay (Bank of Green Bay, Brown County State,

Oneida Land Decision

The U.S. Supreme Court made a major decision that gave hope to members of the Oneida Tribe of Indians living just outside the Green Bay city limits. The court upheld a claim by the Oneida tribe that land they were forced to relinquish to the State of New York nearly 100 years earlier was legally theirs.

Tribal members had been offered ten acres of land in Wisconsin for every acre of land they owned in New York early in the nineteenth century, but just 8 percent accepted the offer. However, in 1892, the remaining Oneidas in New York had their land dispossessed and they were placed in the Onondaga Reservation in New York.

The tribe made its claim for the land in 1912 and was finally getting a decision.

Citizens National, Farmers Exchange, Kellogg National, McCartney National, Peoples Savings & Trust, South Side State, and West Side State) had combined deposits of $9.3 million. The port reported that it annually shipped twenty-two million pounds of cheese, and saw one million tons of coal come and go from the city over the twelve months.

Six streets dominated Green Bay's downtown character, each taking on personalities of their own. Three ran north and south (Washington, Monroe and Broadway) and three ran east and west (Mason, Walnut and Main).

Mason Street was predominantly residential aside from port businesses at the Fox River's edge. East Walnut Street was where most of the professional offices were located, housing doctors, dentists, and lawyers. The Bellin Building and Minahan Building, at opposite corners of the Walnut-Washington intersection, had the highest percentage of them. Aside from one theater, Walnut Street was residential east of Monroe Avenue.

Monroe showed off the homes of many of Green Bay's higher profile families with names such as Straubel, Minahan, Turnbull, Neville, Buchanan, Martin, Lucia, Kittell, Olejniczak and Barkhausen.

But the biggest headache for most community leaders was the presence of roadhouses immediately outside the city limits, mostly

Cold Storage Project

Businesses in Green Bay were anticipating what they thought was the imminent approval and construction of the St. Lawrence Seaway that would bring ocean shipping to the city.

One was Green Bay Warehouse and Cold Storage, which was hurriedly constructing the largest cold storage plant in the Midwest along North Broadway near the intersection with Kellogg Street. The reasoning was that Green Bay would become a great concentration point for all kinds of food once the ocean waterway was completed.

There was also the hope that it would bring more wholesale businesses to Green Bay. As construction of the three-story, 240-foot by 80-foot structure was being built, there was already leased space from Armour Company of Chicago, the Straubel Company of Green Bay, Carpenter-Cook of Marinette, and fruit growers from Door County.

in the town of Preble east of Green Bay's city limits. The word "prostitution" wasn't spoken publicly, but was certainly implied as citizens referred to places where the mores of dress, dance, and drink allegedly were being abused. Many called for the Brown County Board to take action. Minutes of the Board's 1922 meetings provide no evidence that anything was done.

A big problem, some believed, was the type of dancing that was being displayed by the younger generation.

Kline offered a solution.

"Several steps are being taken to require managers of halls to take out municipal licenses," he wrote. "Ordinances provide rules for running the halls. Regulating dancing is far wiser than attempting to stop it. Young people will dance. They see nothing wrong with it. Many dances are wrong. Many are all right."

The city of Madison took more aggressive steps. Its city council passed a regulation requiring all city dance halls to have a supervisor on the dance floor at all times. It also required a matron to be on site whenever there is dancing.

The city leaders also insisted that any youth under eighteen must be accompanied by a chaperone, and once any of the youth or young adults leave the dance hall, they could not return the same night. There had been a push in 1920 to force the roadhouse to close, but it went nowhere despite a *Press-Gazette* editorial that pleaded for "Green Bay to take stock of itself."

Judge Henry Graass, who had donated some of his Door County property for a Boy Scout camp, lectured mothers to train their daughters "not to dress in a manner that causes them to be pointed at with a finger of scorn by men. A girl gone into the world handicapped by ignorance will have a battle ahead. For ignorance is danger and knowledge is shield," he said.

Those seeking entertainment in Green Bay were beginning to respond to the burgeoning motion picture industry, while still patronizing local stage performances and the now declining stream of vaudeville acts booked in the city.

Five movie theaters were in operation – Colonial, Strand, Orpheum, Grand, and Bijou – all on the east side of the Fox River and all but the Orpheum on Washington Street. The Colonial was in the process of a major restoration that would include a large screen to respond to the growing interest in moving pictures.

The top movie stars were becoming familiar to Green Bay residents. Mary Pickford was the star of *Little Lord Fauntleroy* at the Orpheum, while The Bijou had *A Connecticut Yankee in King Arthur's Court*. It cost children a dime and adults thirty-five cents to see the movies.

The most popular books being checked out of the Brown County Library included *If Winter Comes*, by A.S.M. Hutchinson, *Pride of Palomar* by Peter Kyne, *Young Enchanted* by Hugh Walpole, *Journey's End* by Edna Adelaide Brown, and *Queen Victoria* by Lytton Strachey.

All the Packers could do was wait for contact from Joseph Carr, president of the American Football League, to find out if there had been any discussion about the team being reinstated. Nothing came.

Chapter 5

May

Schools and Steetcars

As students neared the end of their school year, concern and even alarm was expressed about the condition of many school buildings and overcrowding. Earl Fisk spoke to the Kiwanis Club and sounded the alarm, noting that only West High School and elementary schools Whitney, Lincoln, and Howe were adequately fireproofed. All other schools were made of brick with wooden frame, and presented serious fire hazards, Fisk said.

Tragedy was averted just three months earlier when schoolchildren playing with matches set fire to Chappell Elementary School at the corner of Fisk Street and Shawano Avenue. The school burned to the ground, with damage estimated at $15,000, but everyone got out safely.

A committee consisting of Fisk, Eben Minahan, Walter Eckhardt, and Frank Buchholz was appointed to work with the School Board to get sprinkler systems installed on the first floor of all school buildings.

Kline wrote in the *Press-Gazette*: "Everyone in Green Bay for many years has known of the unsafe conditions. The city is not in a position at present to replace all these fire traps with modern fireproof buildings, but it can install sprinkler systems and do fire drills.

"We shall be fortunate if we continue to use these buildings until they can be replaced by new and modern structures without a fire disaster. In the meantime, we should not like to be responsible for the consequences that might come from a fire in any of these buildings. Our school houses, as a whole, are perhaps the worst fire hazards in the country, excluding cheap theaters."

Plans were in the works to build a new East High School at the intersection of Baird and Walnut streets, and the School Board approved architectural recommendations that it be adequate for 800 students for at least ten years with an auditorium seating 1,100. The existing East High on South Webster Avenue at Chicago Street would become a junior high school, to be named Washington Junior High.

"It is to be hoped," Kline wrote, "that no expense will be spared in the construction of the new high school to make it absolutely fireproof."

The city had fourteen public elementary schools, one junior high and two high schools. There were also ten parochial elementary schools and one parochial high school – St. Joseph Academy. Overcrowding was bad enough that a one-room, portable classroom was needed outside Mason Elementary School.

Green Bay Fire Department Inspector Capt. James Lester conducted a surprise fire drill at the Cathedral School, and students filed out to the pavement in orderly fashion. Lester then decided to build a fire on the pavement and brought out the school's two chemical

Business Prospects Rising

Signs that the post-war business recession was ending became apparent in Green Bay when industries announced they had a shortage of workers. Any surplus labor had been absorbed and there was a need for farm hands, woodsmen, lumber workers, and railroad construction men. There was also a shortage of female factory workers, and a surplus of stenographers and bookkeepers.

Sale School: It was known as Old Brick and located on Stuart Street next to the First Methodist Church. Built in 1856, it was one of the schools that city officials considered a fire trap in 1922. It was razed in the 1950s. *(Photo courtesy of Neville Public Museum of Brown County)*

---

fire extinguishers to put out the blaze out, but neither of them worked.

It was also a time of labor stress in the public school system. For the first time, teachers were organizing in an effort to increase wages. A union that had been formed two years earlier was striving to increase the annual salary for grade school teachers, which stood at $875. The School Board was reluctant to raise the pay, citing a lack of funds.

Transportation was beginning to have a major impact on Green Bay residents as spring continued. Contracts were awarded to have more streets and roads paved, including one that would connect city residents with Bay Beach.

The business of moving people from one place to another wasn't without controversy. The fears of the late nineteenth century that streetcars would keep farmers away because the cars would frighten their horses had dissipated. Since 1894, city residents were able to get around the city, and even to places outside the city, on a fourteen-car streetcar system that was operated by Wisconsin Public Service. The

Streetcar scene: This city streetcar is seen along North Broadway near the Dousman Street intersection. Operated by Wisconsin Public Service Corp., the streetcars lasted until the late 1930s when they were replaced by a city bus system. *(Photo courtesy of Neville Public Museum of Brown County)*

---

system was regulated and WPS paid an annual fee for the use of the city streets.

It wasn't long before enterprising residents found a way to make money by competing with the streetcar business. Their vehicles were called jitneys – buses – and they began to cut into the streetcar trade, averaging 650 passengers daily. And they were unregulated and didn't pay a fee.

As a result, the City Council passed an ordinance that would prevent the jitneys from operating on any streets that were used by the streetcars and on any streets that had congested intersections. There was also concern that the jitney owners hadn't filed bonds for protection of passengers in case of accident.

One of the jitney owners went to court and obtained a restraining order against the city in order to convince the court that he had a right to do what he was doing and didn't have to come under the city's regulation. Judge Henry Graass backed the city in his decision, setting an annual fee of $100 for those operating jitneys on city streets and imposing the conditions passed by the City Council.

Attorney Timothy Burker, representing the jitney owners, opposed it by insisting that the city was using the excuse of regulating traffic to eliminate competition in the business of transporting passengers.

Kline called Graass's decision and the new ordinance reasonable and equitable.

"The jitneys as they are now operated are a menace to street traffic," he wrote. "They pay no attention to the automobile speed law and pass intersections without slowing down. They are a peril to all vehicular traffic and to pedestrians."

WPS gave passengers a chance to save some money by purchasing streetcar tickets in booklets. You could get four rides for a quarter or fifty rides for $2.50. It would cost WPS $6,000 in lost revenue.

Although the streetcar business would continue for another fifteen years, one company was already cutting back. The Bay Beach Street

Scandal Brewing

Wisconsin Sen. Robert La Follette took the U.S. Senate floor to relay concerns from members of the oil industry about the leasing of some western oil fields to private companies.

Secretary of the Interior Albert Fall, according to a report in the *Wall Street Journal*, leased the Naval Reserves fields to private companies. This included the Teapot Dome oil fields in Wyoming that was leased to Harry Sinclair, owner of one of the largest oil firms in the country, Mammoth Oil Co. La Follette and other senators demanded an investigation into Fall's actions.

Shortly into 1923, Fall resigned in the wake of suspicions that he received bribes in the case. It was disclosed that Fall received $198,000 in Liberty Bonds and $36,000 in cash from Sinclair in exchange for leasing the fields to him.

Teapot Dome would cast a permanent shadow over the administration of President Warren Harding and become the Watergate scandal of its era. Harding's sudden death in August 1923 was attributed by some to the stress that Teapot Dome put on him.

Fall eventually was convicted of taking bribes and sentenced to a year in prison. He served about nine months. Fall died in 1944.

Railway Company that operated a streetcar to Bay Beach decided it wasn't worth it any longer and was prepared to remove the tracks. It was foresight on the company's part, because work was already underway to extend the paved Irwin Street to the Bay Beach grounds.

Lynching Allowed

The U.S. House of Representatives passed an anti-lynching bill after it was revealed that fifty African-Americans had been lynched so far in 1922. But the bill died in the U.S. Senate.

As the populace became more mobile, use of the streetcars diminished. The interurban line between Green Bay and Kaukauna was abandoned in 1928, and the last streetcars were converted to buses by WPS in 1937. The streetcar rails were removed a few years later to provide steel for the war effort.

While the paper industry thrived, so did the dairy business. Brown County was home to sixty-three cheese factories and sixteen creameries, and boasted the largest cheese distribution center in the world. It reported shipping 60,000 tons of cheese annually.

Many other cities were awaiting a decision on a possible pro football franchise for Green Bay. The city of Marinette was one of them, reportedly trying to get Packers player Jab Murray to play for it if the city went ahead and received a franchise.

Chapter 6

June

A New Packers Franchise

Anxiety reigned when the month began as the people hoping to keep pro football in Green Bay still had no guarantees that a Packers franchise would be allowed back in the league. Locally, reorganization was underway, with 250 people meeting at the Beaumont Hotel to discuss the next steps.

The Clair brothers were out of the picture by this time, having returned to Chicago. But everything hinged on a response from the pro league leaders, and no answers had come. Calhoun sent a telegram to league president Joseph Carr, but a return message revealed that Carr was on “an auto tour” and wouldn’t return to his Ohio home for another ten days.

There was reason for optimism, however. Carr had said in January that Green Bay would have an answer to its football fortunes in June and he hinted that the decision would be a positive one for the city. Still, there was no word.

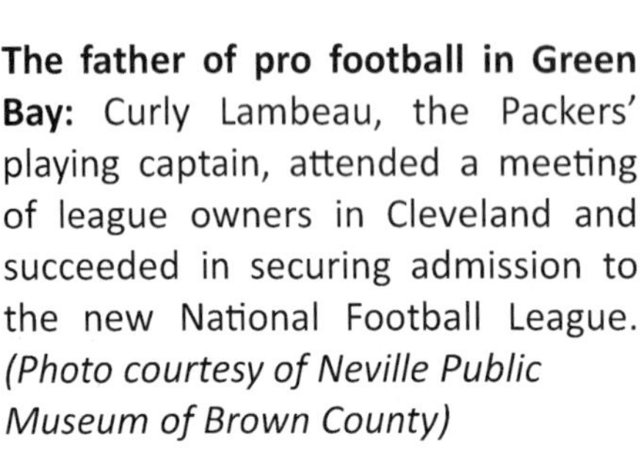

The father of pro football in Green Bay: Curly Lambeau, the Packers' playing captain, attended a meeting of league owners in Cleveland and succeeded in securing admission to the new National Football League. *(Photo courtesy of Neville Public Museum of Brown County)*

Lambeau described the urgency.

"If we don't lay a foundation here we will be out of luck in getting together a team which will enable the Bay to keep its prominent place on the football map," he said in a comment likely penned by Calhoun.

A week later, Carr sent a telegram to Calhoun indicating that no action had been taken on the Packers' petition for a franchise because the league managers and board of directors hadn't met since January. But he said a league meeting was planned for later in the month in Cleveland and suggested the Packers have some representatives there.

"Assuring you that I consider Green Bay one of the best football towns in the Middle West," Carr wired. He was encouraged to learn the Clair brothers were no longer involved and he planned to introduce new bylaws aimed at keeping teams from dipping into the college amateur ranks to find players.

Calhoun sounded the trumpet of hope.

"Football fans will welcome the news that the American Football League hasn't entirely forgotten about Green Bay and the application of the Bay city in the pro league will be given due consideration at the summer meeting of the gridiron magnates," he wrote. "Green Bay went to the front so fast in professional football last fall that it would be an unfortunate step if they were forced to remain outside of the big league football."

The meeting of more than twenty pro team owners took place June 24-25 at the Hollenden Hotel in Cleveland. In addition to the sixteen cities still part of the American Football League, there were representatives from eight other cities – New Haven, Connecticut; Duluth, Minnesota; Sioux City, Iowa; Toledo and Youngstown, Ohio; and Milwaukee, Green Bay, and Racine, Wisconsin – that sought franchises.

A major topic of discussion was the use of college players. The league owners agreed to outlaw the practice, with the first violation incurring a $500 fine and a second violation raising the possibility of expulsion from the league. The rule would have an impact on the Milwaukee Badgers, who were caught three years later playing four high school youths. Facing the fine, the team disbanded.

League owners also voted to give Carr the authority to assign referees to league games as a step toward eliminating favoritism.

Lambeau attended for the Packers and paid $250 to submit the team's application for a franchise. He was accompanied to Cleveland by his friend, Donald Murphy, whose family was in the real estate business. Murphy had sold his Marmon Roadster for $1,500 and gave Lambeau $200 to help meet the $250 re-entry fee. In exchange, Lambeau let Murphy play in one game later that season.

Lambeau promised the owners that no college players would again play for the Packers and that a complete housecleaning had taken place among the Packers' leadership, himself not included, of course.

By the end of the meeting, Green Bay, Milwaukee, Toledo, and Racine were admitted to the league. The owners also granted a franchise to George Halas, who was forming the Chicago Bears, having given up the Decatur Staleys. Team owners also voted to change the name of the league from American Professional Football Association to the National Football League.

Calhoun beat the drum for Wisconsin.

"It looks as if Wisconsin will soon run Ohio a close race for professional football activities. For years, Canton, Columbus and Cleveland ruled supreme but it may be a different story this fall."

Comments attributed to Lambeau had a Calhoun sound to them.

"One thing is sure. The football magnates all over the country take their hats off to Green Bay as a football town."

A news report out of Cleveland assessed the Milwaukee situation, although not by today's politically correct standards.

"As yet the outlook for the Milwaukee club is a bit cloudy but those behind the club have promised a good team," it read. "An attempt was made to sign up Jim Thorpe, famous Indian star, to coach and captain the team but it was made known at the meeting in Cleveland last week that the redskin would lead the New York Nationals, a pro team to play in the Polo Grounds in Gotham."

Although football continued to be a hot topic in Green Bay all month, it couldn't displace baseball as the most popular sport to most fans. The majority of the most famous pro athletes were baseball players and household names – George Sisler, Rogers Hornsby, Ty Cobb, Tris Speaker, Babe Ruth – and their careers were followed closely.

This was less than three years after several members of the Chicago White Sox conspired to intentionally lose the 1919 World Series to the Cincinnati Reds in order to earn a payoff from professional gamblers. Although acquitted of charges of conspiracy to defraud, seven members of the "Black Sox," were banned from baseball for life by Commissioner Kenesaw Mountain Landis.

The Black Sox scandal was still big news after 1922 as baseball continued to be the nation's most popular sport. Many of the former White Sox players continued to play sandlot ball in communities throughout the United States – mostly under assumed names – and were never reinstated in organized baseball.

Two of them – Eddie Cicotte and Swede Risberg – played in a game for Appleton, Wisconsin, in the Valley Baseball League on June 11. Immediately, the president of the Oshkosh team said the players wouldn't be allowed in that city's ballpark.

Diabetes Advancement

A fourteen-year-old Toronto boy became the first person to have a successful insulin treatment of diabetes. Leonard Thompson had been near death when he was given the insulin developed in 1921 by Frederick Banting and Charles Best. Thompson's full recovery proved that the insulin was successful.

League officials met four days later and told the Appleton team organizers to clean up their act or they would lose their franchise. They said any team using the banned players would face serious consequences.

Cicotte, the pitcher whose confession blew the lid off the scandal a year after the World Series fix, pitched in some games in Louisiana and later in Illinois. He eventually became a game warden in Michigan and a mechanic at the Detroit Ford plant, but never attended another major league game. Biographers wrote that his conscience is what prompted him to confess and his friends described him as a fine person who made a big mistake. Cicotte died in 1969.

Risberg continued to play sandlot baseball for ten years after being spotted playing for Appleton. Later, he ran a dairy farm and eventually needed to have a leg amputated, which doctors said was the result of spiking he received as a player. Known to be one of the ringleaders of the gambling scandal in 1919, Risberg committed a World Series record eight errors in the series. He died in 1975 as the last remaining member of the Black Sox.

Some of the former White Sox didn't even try to hide their identities. The team picture of the Wittenberg (Wis.) Grays team included George "Buck" Weaver, one of the Black Sox. In case anyone didn't recognize him, he was wearing his old White Sox jersey.

More and more automobiles were appearing on city and county streets, so the County Board acted to keep speed under control. It hired Joseph Reinhard, Henry Servais, and Charles Glawe as traffic patrolmen to start writing tickets for those driving too fast. However, they were apparently too eager, prompting representatives of the Board to complain that Green Bay was gaining a reputation as a speed trap. The Board did lay down the law on vehicles without lights, however, passing an ordinance that required vehicles on the public roads to have lights on thirty minutes after sunset and thirty minutes before sunrise, or incur a $10 fine.

The city took advantage of the bulging automobile market by sponsoring an Automobile Day to include parades of cars and other events. It was set for the second Saturday of the month, but nearly two inches of rain the night before forced a one-week postponement as the roads outside the city took too much of a beating to make driving safe.

The storm created many problems for the city. The East River overflowed its banks for the first time in thirty-one years. Chickens and cattle on the Albert Cornellison farm on Dixon Road were swept away by the river's current. Residents near the river on Mason Street were forced out of their homes. The Main Street Bridge over the Fox River was closed because of the high water. Crop damage was heavy, train service was temporarily suspended, and even telephone lines were affected.

More than 300 feet of concrete was washed away south of the city on the new Highway 15, which later would become Highway 41 and be rerouted around the cities it initially passed through. Many sheds and outhouses were destroyed in what was called the biggest storm to hit the city since June 1914.

The new Holy Apostles Episcopal Church in Oneida was consecrated by the diocesan bishop after three days of rain, but many villagers couldn't go directly to the site because by then 4.33 inches of rain had fallen and Duck Creek isolated one side of the community from the other. Many parishioners took a circuitous route through Green Bay or Freedom to get to the church.

Automobile Day finally took place with a parade of cars motoring down Mason Street from the east.

With auto traffic increasing, residents on South Broadway petitioned the city to pave the blocks between Fifth and Seventh streets. City Councilman Frank Cormier admitted it was probably the worst piece of road in the city, but warned that it would cost $18,000.

According to the residents, pedestrians were getting splashed by mud from autos, bicycles, and horse teams because there was sidewalk on just one side of the road. Temporary improvements were planned, but permanent paving would have to wait.

Mayor Wiesner declared a half-holiday for the city during the last week of the month to celebrate the season opening of Bay Beach.

Fred Rahr was sentenced to eight months incarceration and fined $15,000 after his conviction on fifty counts of selling beer with alcohol contents between 1.25 and 2.58 percent. His attorney said the brewery was driven to manufacturing beer of illegal strength because of the keen competition.

Finally, six young men from Green Bay left for Camp Custer in western Wisconsin to participate in a program called Citizen Training, preparation for the military. One of them was Austin Straubel, 109 S. Monroe St., whose name eventually would be tied to the Green Bay airport.

Good Boating on Goodell Street: This was about the only mode of transportation near the East River in May and June 1922 when floods covered the streets. The winter of 1921-22 was noted for several blizzards resulting in a heavy layer of snow. By spring, the heavy runoff from the snow followed by torrential rains caused major flooding. The East River's flooding covered large parts of East Mason, Crooks, and Goodell Streets, as well as other portions of streets in the area. *(Photo courtesy of Neville Public Museum of Brown County)*

Chapter 7

July

New Parks and Labor Strife

The city's face experienced another upgrade as summer settled on Green Bay. A trend to develop city parks that would serve the public for generations continued.

Wilbur D. Fisk, who had operated a successful land and lumber business, donated twelve and a half acres of land between Dousman and Reed streets on the west side to the city for use as a recreational park. The park was named in memory of Fisk's son, Hiram, who died of the flu while serving in the army during World War I.

Fisk established a trust fund, into which he donated $5,000 for maintenance and development of the park. He told Mayor Wiesner that he initially planned to include the donation of land in his will, but decided to do it immediately since land values were getting higher and available park space was becoming scarce.

This was the third such donation to the city in a three-year period. In 1920, Mitchell Joannes, a member of the family that operated a

Bay Beach: The Bay Beach pavilion is shown in this early spring aerial view. The family amusement park started primarily as a beach attraction, with rides added in later years. The park remains one of the drawing cards for Green Bay today. *(Photo courtesy of Neville Public Museum of Brown County)*

---

successful food distribution business in the city, donated forty acres of land on the city's east side. It became Joannes Park.

The same year, Frank Murphy and Fred Rahr donated eleven acres of land that was known as Bay View Park along the bayshore. This became Bay Beach. It was there that Mayor Wiesner predicted the blossoming of a tourist attraction for the city.

"The success of the municipal experiences has convinced city officials that 1922 will be a banner year and every possible attempt will be made to bring out that the beach is an ideal place for picnic and bathing parties," he said.

Late in the month, a concrete road was finally extended from Main Street to Bay Beach and beginning with North Irwin Street.

A *Press-Gazette* editorial hailed the beach's potential.

"Bay Beach stands out as one of the conspicuous achievements of the present city government," it proclaimed. "A great change has been wrought and it is all for the better. Not only has it made Bay Beach a really delightful place, but it has laid the foundation for making it one of the most beautiful spots on the bay and one of the most valuable municipal parks in Wisconsin."

Bay Beach continued to be a popular swimming spot for a generation and the site was annexed to the city in 1929, with an additional eight acres added to the acreage donated by Murphy and Rahr between 1933 and 1948.

A streetcar carried bathers and picnickers from downtown Green Bay and a bathhouse was added in 1930, but pollution forced the swimming beach to be shut down in 1933. The park was leased to private individuals until 1950 when it was taken over by the city's recreation department.

A new roller coaster was built in 1929 to replace the one torn down in 1922, but it had to be dismantled in 1936 because of insurance issues. The following month, the streetcar from the city to Bay Beach would carry 15,644 patrons.

The month was dominated by labor strife in the United States and had a significant impact on Green Bay. Seven of the sixteen railroad labor unions voted to go on strike July 1 because of wage cuts imposed by the Railroad Labor Board.

The inflation that fueled the economy during World War I was countered after the war as price levels returned to normal and many former soldiers entered the work force. Anti-union sentiment in the conservative administration of President Warren Harding led to a 12 percent wage and benefit reduction to rail employees. But the Labor Board managed to split union forces, promising the largest rail unions – those that covered engineers, firemen and conductors – that they wouldn't see their benefits cut any further.

That left the shopmen and maintenance workers to carry on against the government efforts to cut wages. It affected 400,000 union employees nationally, 100,000 in Chicago alone, and 650 in Green Bay. On July 1, 350 employees of the St. Paul line, 175 of the Green Bay & Western, and thirteen from the Chicago and North Western walked off the job. They marched together to Turner Hall at the corner of Monroe Avenue and Walnut Street. It included car repairmen, mechanics, boilermakers, track repairmen, roundhouse men, and oilers.

Kline wrote that the shopmen were taking too much of the blame for the labor strife.

"The present reduction has too much of the appearance of passing the cost of the rate adjustments to labor. It is quite clear that labor ought not to bear the entire sacrifice of lower freight rates, granted even that it should bear any. If it is necessary to reduce costs to meet the reductions, there are other fields. We think the public at large and many shippers are of the opinion that there is sufficient opportunity for retrenchment in railroad operations, and enterprise in railroad management to bring this business up to a paying basis without putting the burden on labor."

Samuel Cady, attorney for the Chicago and North Western Railroad, saw things differently.

"Some wanted an excuse to strike, some because of the Labor Board's decision, but thousands upon thousands because they were afraid not to strike because of physical violence or social ostracism." Trains stayed on schedule despite the strike, and local rail officials said they wouldn't hire strikebreakers.

Still, there was pressure on other rail employees. Alphonse Basteyna, who lived at 308 Mather St., continued to go to work as a foreman in the North Western shops. Several striking North Western shopmen went to Basteyna's house and were told by his wife, Elizabeth, that he was at work.

"He is at work, is he?" one of the men said. "Don't you know the risk of having your house blown up? You better tell him to stay home where he is safe or he'll get a good trimming by seven or eight of us fellows."

Sister to the Rescue

Three-year-old Lorraine Pierner was holding a sparkler as she sat on her family porch at 114 N. Clay St. on the Fourth of July. The lit sparkler slipped out of her hand and set fire to the calico apron she was wearing. Lorraine screamed and started running down the street.

Her thirteen-year-old sister, Evelyn, ran after her and caught her, first rolling her on the grass, then grabbing a rug off the porch and wrapping her in it. Lorraine suffered burns but survived.

Evelyn was hailed as a heroine.

Working on the railroad: A Chicago and North Western Railroad crew poses with a steam engine. A railroad strike involving shopmen and maintenance workers was a major labor story in Green Bay and throughout the nation in 1922. *(Photo courtesy of Neville Public Museum of Brown County)*

The threat prompted the Basteynas to seek, and get, a temporary injunction against North Western strikers, preventing them from picketing the company shops.

Stephen Nowakowski was also a foreman at the North Western shops, and he chose to eat and sleep on company property rather than go home to his wife and five children. Strikers showed up at his house, however, and told his wife they were getting the number of scabs' houses so "we can put a bomb under it."

Rudolph Loche didn't strike and stayed on his North Western job as a foreman in the car repair shops. He also stayed on company property so he didn't have to cross the picket lines, but on Sunday, August 19, he decided to visit his wife and five children. Three strikers – two of them members of city or county law enforcement – confronted him outside his house and searched him for weapons, finding none.

A week later, Loche and fellow employee Frank Boyce hired a Yellow Cab to take them home for Sunday visits with their families. But strikers stopped the cab at the plant entrance, pulled Loche and Boyce from the vehicle and beat them.

Attorney Cady was appalled at the absence of response by police.

"It seems incredible in the year of our Lord nineteen hundred and twenty-two, and in enlightened United States of America, groups of men could go about putting wives and mothers in fear for the personal safety of their loved ones and the incidents go unheeded by civil authorities."

The strike failed, due mostly to intervention by the federal government. Attorney General Harry Daugherty convinced President Harding that the strike was resulting in excessive violence. Harding's Secretary of Commerce, Herbert Hoover, insisted that the unions had some legitimate grievances.

But Daugherty, who would soon become the target of fraud accusations in unrelated issues, was able to persuade Federal Judge James Wilkerson to issue a sweeping injunction against the workers, forbidding them to picket, give interviews, or gather. The government hired 2,200 U.S. Marshalls to enforce the injunction. Daugherty argued that "the survival and supremacy of the government of the United States" was at stake.

By mid-September, the strike dissolved and most of the Green Bay strikers returned to work. The sixty-eight-day strike left the shopmen at 65 cents per hour. In all, the Green Bay area strikers lost a total of $398,000 from the work stoppage.

The entire episode left a bad taste for many strikers and observers.

Wrote Kline: "Whatever the mysterious purpose of the government has been, it had all the appearance of a move to break the strike in favor of the railroads. The more the act of the Attorney General is studied, the more it looks like a blow aimed at labor unions, a move to support the open shop and an attempt to help the railroads win the strike. It was repulsive to the American conception of fair play. There cannot be the slightest question that the wording of the injunction abridges constitutional rights and privileges."

The only consolation the unions eventually took from the strike was the fact that it planted the seeds for the 1926 Railroad Labor Act that guided the industry for future decades.

Safely back into pro football's good graces, Lambeau set out to get players under contract. One of the first to sign was big lineman

Cub Buck, who was working as a Boy Scout director in Appleton after his first season with the Packers. His contract included a provision that he would practice three times a week.

Flight Distance Record

Two army pilots, Lt. Oakley Kelley and Lt. John MacReady, set a world record when they flew 2,060 miles non-stop from San Diego to Indianapolis. They might have flown farther but had to land when the plane's radiator sprung a leak.

Lambeau went after three Marinette athletes: Jab Murray, Buff Wagner, and Sammy Powers. It was significant to the Marinette-Menominee community as it was waiting to see what Green Bay did before deciding if it would try to develop a team. It never did.

The league followed up its June meeting by announcing that any team caught playing college players would be fined from $250-$1,000 and likely face dismissal from the league. Each team was required to send a $1,000 check to the league secretary in Ohio that would be kept on file, just in case.

Joe Carr also said the league would begin to appoint neutral officials for each game, and asked each franchise to forward names of two officials. Green Bay submitted the names of former University of Wisconsin captain Joe Hoeffel and St. Norbert football coach George Carey.

A possible problem was emerging for Chicago's franchise and would be discussed by team presidents at an August meeting. A franchise had been granted to George Halas, who surrendered the Staleys franchise and named his new one the Bears. But former Staleys manager Bill Harley announced that he should have the franchise that was given to Halas and even leased White Sox Park for games in 1922.

Carr also predicted pro football would become as popular as college football and that record attendance was expected in the upcoming season.

Chapter 8

August

A Highway for the Ages

No event that spoke to the future was more significant than the official opening of Highway Trunk 15, the cement highway that went from the Illinois border to Green Bay and continued to Michigan's Upper Peninsula. It opened the roadways to greater travel and more business with the other cities along the route including Appleton, Neenah, Oshkosh, Fond du Lac, Milwaukee, Racine, and Kenosha.

The highway came as a result of state officials recognizing the growing impact of the automobile, a recognition that really began in 1905 when the State Legislature first agreed to budget state funds for highways. Voters approved a constitutional amendment in 1908 that allowed the state to provide funds for road improvements, and passage of the State Aid Act of 1911 permitted counties to bond for county road improvements.

Racine, Ozaukee, Dodge, Fond du Lac and Brown counties went ahead and bonded – Brown County for $2.5 million – and it was estimated the highway cost about $25,000 per mile. The state highway department estimated that the 180-mile stretch from the Illinois border to just north of Green Bay required 5,400 train cars of sand, 10,800 cars of stone and gravel, and 2,800 cars of cement.

Highway improvements were particularly welcome to farmers in rural Brown County. Better roads made it easier to get their products to market, allowed the consolidation of several one-room schoolhouses, and gave rural residents better access to public health services.

Businesses hailed the highway's opening, and city and county officials began to take a harder look at the potential for tourism in Green Bay.

Highway 15 was first designated in 1918 when route numbers were assigned throughout the state. When the U.S. Highway System was installed in 1926, Highway 15 became Highway 41, and State Highway 16 from Chippewa Falls to Green Bay became Highway 29. The same highway became Highway 141 from Green Bay to Manitowoc.

The opening of Highway 141 was a particular boon to Main Street businesses as it added another major thoroughfare to share the street. The automobile was fast becoming the mode of travel as well as a sign of financial security in the state. License fee collections in Brown

Car dealership: Salesmen for the Green Bay Motor Car Company pose for this early 1920s photograph. Located at 316-318 North Jefferson Street, the company was a distributor of Maxwell and Chalmers automobiles. *(Photo courtesy of Neville Public Museum of Brown County)*

Ireland's Michael Collins Assassinated

Michael Collins, a leader for Irish independence and one of the negotiators for the Anglo-Irish Treaty in 1921, was assassinated August 22 by extremists after he left a meeting in Cork.

Collins was the finance director of the newly established Irish Free State and had been a member of Sinn Fein, the political wing for Irish independence. When he signed the treaty, he said he was signing his own death warrant.

County went from $60,714 in 1920, to $75,395 in 1921, to $88,180 in 1922.

There were twelve auto dealers in Green Bay when Highway 15 opened. The new Essex cost $1,295 while a Studebaker went for $1,650. You could buy a new four-door Maxwell sedan for $1,335 and a coupe for $1,235 at Green Bay Motors in the third block of North Jefferson Street. The Overland Sales Company on West Walnut Street was selling its Overland sedan for $895.

The impact on highway construction was obvious as thirty-one miles of road were paved in Brown County during the year. It also put the streetcar business on the dying list, although the last one wouldn't disappear from Green Bay for another fifteen years.

While the opening of Highway 15 was a one-time occasion, the Northeast Wisconsin Fair in De Pere was an annual event that dominated the last week of August and the start of September. A record 18,000 people attended on one day and the number of vendors was an all-time high. All Green Bay municipal workers were given a half-day off so they could attend the fair.

The only blemish was a massive thunderstorm that dumped 2.5 inches of rain on the fairgrounds as stock car races were set to begin one evening. Patrons raced for their cars and a logjam resulted at the gate, but no casualties were reported.

Another popular event that was drawing more and more people was the evening dance at Bay Beach. The dances were held two times each week, and the park department was considering adding a third night.

Northeast Wisconsin Fair: This was a common site in August when much of the city shut down to allow residents to enjoy the Northeast Wisconsin Fair at the Brown County Fairgrounds in De Pere. This was Green Bay Day at the fair. Note the mix of horse-drawn carriages (front right) and motorcars in the photo. *(Photo courtesy of Neville Public Museum of Brown County)*

The railroad strike wasn't the only labor issue that had a significant impact on Green Bay in 1922. Coal miners in Pennsylvania and West Virginia, who were dissatisfied with the rollback of wages to the 1919 levels and eager to form unions, went on strike. This affected 610,000 miners and set the course for coal shortages that would continue into the following year.

One result was that tonnage shipped down the Fox River from the cities to the south would drop from 285,000 tons in 1921 to 210,000 tons in 1922 because of a coal shortage. Coal coming into the Green Bay harbor from the lakes dropped from 675,000 tons in 1921 to 562,000 tons the following year.

A few boatloads were still arriving as autumn drew closer, but businesses and families dependent on coal were being advised to conserve. The miners returned to work before summer ended, but the federal fuel distribution committee said it would be impossible to give the Great Lakes region more than 50 percent of its normal supply of hard coal in the upcoming winter.

Green Bay was predominantly Republican politically. But the dominating political figure in the state, Sen. Robert La Follette – himself a Republican – made many of the party faithful uncomfortable.

That's because La Follette, known as "Fighting Bob," was a rogue Republican, having gained his reputation as a social reformer that launched the Progressive movement.

Advertising Successes

As radio became more popular, more companies produced ads to sell their products. Palmolive Soap claimed it could provide a school-girl complexion and Lucky Strike cigarettes insisted it could protect the throat from excessive coughing.

The *Press-Gazette* was not in his corner, using its editorial page to write "Mr. La Follette is not only a political outlaw in the Senate but is in personal seclusion. He has broken with the party. He stands alone."

La Follette gave a two-hour speech at the Armory after being introduced by Green Bay attorney John Reynolds, who said, "If he isn't elected our next president, he ought to be."

He would be re-elected easily to the U.S. Senate in the November election. La Follette ran unsuccessfully for president in 1924 on the Progressive ticket and died a few months later in 1925.

There were four political parties functioning in the Green Bay area as the elections neared. The Republicans and Democrats were joined by the Prohibition and Socialist parties. The Republicans were led by Ole Hansen of Denmark and Joe Lazansky of Kewaunee. The Democratic leadership came from James Hughes of De Pere and George Keller of Appleton. Maria Nelson of Green Bay headed the 9th District's (it became the 8th District later) Prohibition Party, and John Everhard of Green Bay led the Socialists.

Judge Henry Graass tried to unseat U.S. Rep. George Schneider of Appleton and had the backing of the *Press-Gazette* editorial page. But that meant Graass had to first defeat Schneider in the Republican primary election, which he almost did. Schneider won by 109 votes. When he came up short, Graass decided to run as an independent Democrat in the November election. He lost again because too few Republican voters were willing to cross the political aisle.

Chapter 9

September

Fall Means Football

The World War was still in the recent past and many veterans were banking on a veterans' compensation bill – known as the Bonus Bill – that would help them in the heavy unemployment post-war days. It was a political football that was tossed around during election season. By the time Congress took up the issue, thirty-eight states agreed to pay bonuses. The Senate proposed that every veteran would receive $1.25 for each day of overseas service during the war and $1.00 for every day of domestic service. They proposed quarterly payments and gave soldiers the option of receiving compensation through life insurance.

The debate had the attention of veterans in Northeast Wisconsin – 2,696 from Brown County had served in the army during the war and 331 had been in the navy. The Bonus Bill had strong backing from the newly formed American Legion, whose commander, Hanford MacNider, met with President Harding to lobby for his reluctant support.

Forgiveness

Roy Vanden Busch was a thirteen-year-old paper delivery boy for the *Press-Gazette* when he was struck by a car on a city street and died from the injuries. The driver, James Kehoe, fled the scene but arrested later and faced serious charges.

But Kehoe tried to raise money to compensate the boy's family. When the case came before Judge Nicholas J. Monahan, Roy's father asked that the charges against Kehoe be dismissed, saying he found no room in his heart for vengeance. Kehoe was ordered to pay the father $250 for lost wages when he was away from work and to cover funeral expenses.

Editorially, the *Press-Gazette* took up the cause.

"Patriotism is a noble virtue and it was gloriously exemplified in the World War, as in every other war in which America has fought. But it cannot live on air alone even when that air is heated. It thrives on bread and butter as well as on subtle emotions. With thousands of ex-servicemen walking the streets of cities looking for work, it would be asking a good deal of them not to elect the cash bonus in any plan of adjusted compensation.

"In the face of such a situation, it is also asking a little too much of them to forego their obvious rights and simple justice in order that theoretically those who have prospered in the past may prosper a little more in the future. Is it the ex-serviceman alone who shall make sacrifices to ameliorate the burdens of the war?"

But the country faced a financial crisis and the thought of paying billions of dollars to veterans and raising the national debt dragged the issue through the political caucuses. The Bonus Bill was opposed by big business interests.

Kline called them out in his editorials.

"The financial and large commercial interests of the country are fighting this expenditure. Their plea is that the country cannot afford it, that it will impose an unjust burden on the people, meaning primarily themselves. It does so in the spirit of selfishness. If we had red-blooded American citizens in control of Congress they would snap their fingers in the face of the organized opposition promptly and enact the necessary legislation."

Harding even made the startling move of showing up in Congress during a special session to urge defeat of the Bonus Bill, repeating that the country just couldn't afford it. This angered many senators, including La Follette. The House passed the bill 333-70 and the Senate followed with a 36-17 favorable vote.

Harding vetoed it, the House overrode his veto, but the Senate sustained it.

The Bonus Bill would reappear two years later on President Calvin Coolidge's desk, and he would veto it as well. It wasn't until 1932 that a Bonus Bill was passed and signed, with veterans entitled to benefits by 1945.

None of this mattered to Albert Watermolen, a thirty-one-year-old veteran of Battery B who was gassed during combat in France during the war. He died at his home on Elm Street as the political debate raged.

The Sullivan Post in Green Bay was one of 350 posts in Wisconsin. Its first commander, James McGillan, stressed the importance of action.

"We are standing to one side and letting men be elected to office who are absolutely unfit for such office. And as long as we are doing this, we are failing in our duties as citizens."

The newly formed Green Bay Football Club submitted its Articles of Organization to Register of Deeds Frank Smith at mid-month, with Lambeau as president, Joseph Ordens as vice president, Nathan Abrams as treasurer, and George Calhoun as secretary.

Lambeau was busy recruiting players and started practice on September 5 at Joannes Park. The league schedule was announced and the Packers' first game was October 1 at Rock Island.

Lambeau decided to schedule a non-league game against the Duluth K.C.'s, a team that had beaten the Minneapolis club late in 1921. The game was set for September 24 and the Packers were buoyed by the knowledge that Charlie Mathys, a former Green Bay West and

"Get (Charlie) Mathys and we'll have a forward passing combination second to none. With Mathys on the receiving end and Lambeau tossing 'em, our aerial attack will be the equal to any team in the country."
- Packers star Cub Buck

Indiana University football star, agreed to come home and play for his hometown team.

That delighted the Packers' Cub Buck.

"Get Mathys and we'll have a forward passing combination second to none. With Mathys on the receiving end and Lambeau tossing 'em, our aerial attack will be the equal to any team in the country," Buck said.

The Duluth team was bolstered by the signing of "Ink" Marshall, identified as "the famous colored end."

The game was to be played in Duluth and many Packers took the overnight train from Neenah to Duluth, arriving at 8:30 the morning of the game.

It didn't go well for the Packers. One of Lambeau's passes was intercepted by former Notre Dame star Denny Coughlin, who ran fifty-five yards for the game's only touchdown. The Packers got a safety when the Duluth punter fumbled the snap in his own end zone, and the game came down to the Packers' final drive in the closing minutes. A pass interference call against Duluth would have given the Packers the ball at the hosts' 1-yard-line but, according to the game report from Duluth, a referee from the host city by the name of Vaughn nullified the penalty by calling a holding penalty on the Packers. Then the game ended.

When it was over, Packers officials got a verbal commitment from the K.C.'s coach to play a game in Green Bay later in the year.

Calhoun wrote that every cloud has a silver lining and the game provided two. For one, it wasn't a league game. And two, the Duluth management seemed agreeable to coming to Green Bay for a return match on Thanksgiving Day. The only thing that would prevent it was the contract the Packers had signed to play the Chicago Bears that day.

The Packers looked ahead to their first league game the following Sunday at Rock Island. They sought someone to scrimmage and found them in the Lawrence College football team.

Noteworthy at the end of the month was the death of 105-year-old James Bell of Abrams. A native of Ireland, he was born in 1817 – when Thomas Jefferson and John Adams were still alive – and had just celebrated his 105th birthday. Among the mourners was his wife, Louise, 103.

A Day at the Game: Cars pack the parking lot at Hagemeister Park on the city's east side, the home field for the Green Bay Packers. A small ticket booth and a handful of people in line can be seen in front of the far right end of the white sign on the building.

(Photo courtesy of Neville Public Museum of Brown County)

Chapter 10

October

Support Grows for the Packers

Football still wasn't the most popular sport in Green Bay. The top story on the front page of the *Press-Gazette* the entire first week of the month – getting better play than the coal strike, the upcoming elections, and the efforts to raise money for a YMCA – was the baseball World Series between the New York Giants and New York Yankees.

The Packers were back in action the first Sunday of the month, playing their first league game at Rock Island, Illinois. The Islanders won 19-14 behind running back Jimmy Conzelman. He drop-kicked a 25-yard field goal and his running staked Rock Island to a 19-7 lead. Green Bay closed it to the final score when Paddy Cronin caught a touchdown pass from Lambeau. The Packers had one last chance in the closing minutes, but Lambeau's long fourth-down pass to Cowboy Wheeler was batted away at the last second.

Calhoun's account of the game in the *Press-Gazette* was far from downbeat. He wrote that many of the Green Bay fans who traveled to the game "considered the result nearly as good as a victory."

Later in the week, he cited a compliment from league President Joe Carr.

"Evidently, Green Bay's fame as a football town is not alone confined to Wisconsin," Calhoun wrote. "President Carr called the 'Bay' one of the best pigskin communities in the country. The honor is justly deserved, however, because in the past four years Green Bay has mounted the pigskin ladder of fame until it now is pretty close to the top. Nothing succeeds like success and Green Bay appears to be thriving immediately on its gridiron progressiveness."

At that point, the Packers were 0-2 and preparing for its first home game. It would be against the Racine Legion. Calhoun still referred to the Packers as the Bay or Big Blue, noting the color of the team's jerseys.

Predicting a crowd of 4,000, tickets were being sold at the Beaumont Hotel, The Congress Billiard Room, Bobby Lynch's Billiard Hall, Schweger Drug, Bokel's Drug, and an establishment called McDonald's in De Pere that sold something, but not hamburgers.

The Racine team was feeling pretty good after holding the Chicago Bears to a 6-0 score in their first-week loss. Reports out of Racine indicated that fifteen buses were booked to make the trip to Green Bay for the game.

The *Press-Gazette* published a four-page advertising section promoting the game and local businesses, with photos of players in each ad. Calhoun didn't run out of material to pump up the game. He pointed out that the Green Bay team included seven Green Bay natives: Curly Lambeau, Eddie Glick, Joe Secord, Fee Klaus, Cowboy Wheeler, Charlie Mathys, and Martin Zoll. He wrote that "never before has there been so much football talk in the air."

Lambeau said, "You can tell the fans we're ready. I think we'll beat Racine."

Only they didn't. Racine won 10-6.

"If they can shake the hoodoo, there is no question they will prove a mean foe," Calhoun wrote. The game drew about 3,000 fans.

Again, a last-second pass fell incomplete, this time from Lambeau to Glick in the end zone. Green Bay got its lone touchdown when Cub Buck blocked a punt and Wheeler recovered it in the end zone. Lambeau's dropkick for the extra point hit the upright.

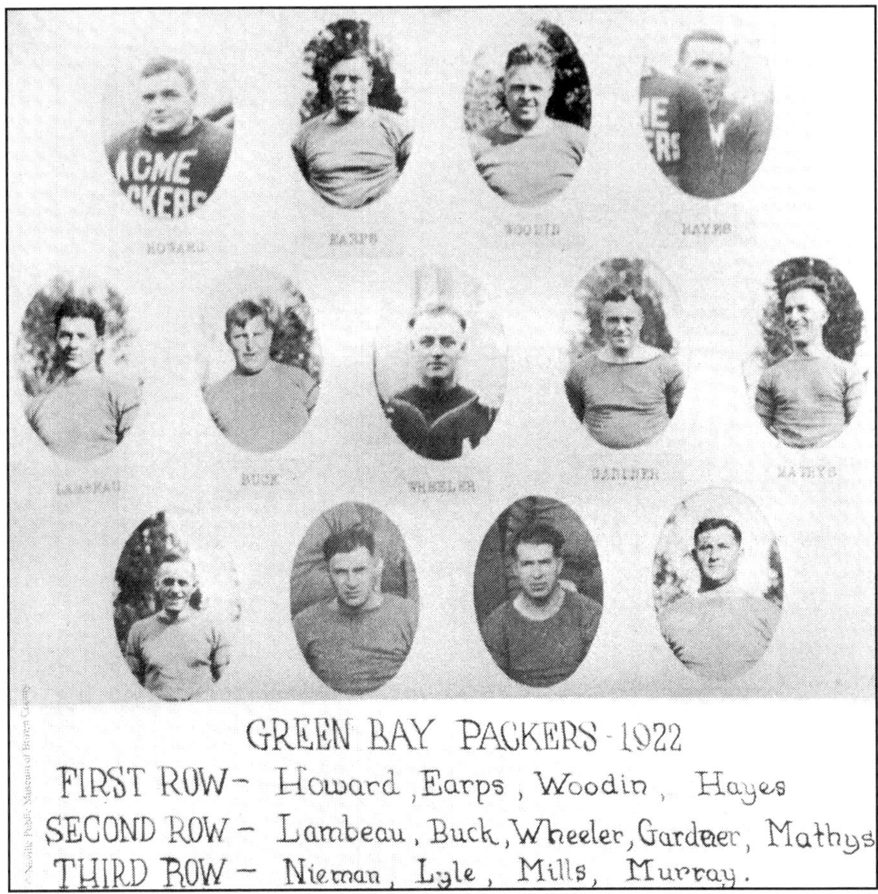

The 1922 Packers: Top - Lynn Howard, Jug Earp (misspelled in picture), Whitey Wooden, Dave Hayes; Middle - Curly Lambeau, Cub Buck, Lyle Wheeler, Moose Gardner, Charlie Mathys; Bottom - Walter Nieman, Dewey Lyle, Stan Mills, Jab Murray. *(Photo courtesy Neville Public Museum of Brown County)*

"It was a bad 14 minutes for a person with a weak heart," wrote Calhoun of the fourth quarter.

Football promotion was nearing a frenetic state despite the three straight losses to begin the season, a stretch that Calhoun dismissed by suggesting"there is a jinx somewhere around the Bay eleven."

He remained unbowed in the face of citizen complaints about the team's record.

"The thrice of upsets, one right after another, handed Lambeau's aggregation hasn't set very well with the followers of the Bay eleven and in many instances the anvil chorus is bursting forth loudly. A victory will shut this up in a jiffy and the players, realizing the condition of things at home, can be counted on to battle doubly hard to break into the win column. There are hundreds of loyal fans around these parts who are sticking with the team through defeat."

Calhoun said the three losses spread "gobs of gloom," in the city.

Next on the schedule were the Chicago Cardinals, who boasted probably the best player in the league, Paddy Driscoll. The game was set to be played in Chicago, but the site wouldn't be known until the day before the game. The baseball Chicago Cubs were engaged in their annual season-ending game against the White Sox, and a victory by the White Sox would mean the Packers and Cardinals couldn't use White Sox Stadium. The Sox did win, 2-0, forcing the football game to be relocated to Normal Park at the corner of 61st Street and Racine Avenue.

Again, Lambeau was confident, saying "Every man on the squad is in good shape and I think we are going to break into the win column."

Again, he was wrong. The Cardinals dominated and won 16-3, and Driscoll was as good as advertised.

Calhoun's story referred to the two Horween brothers "playing under the name of McMahon" with one of them scoring twice on the "Harvard criss-cross play." The only Green Bay score came on Charlie Mathys's dropkick field goal.

> **New Perfume**
>
> Coco Chanel introduces Chanel No. 5, which will become the world's best-known perfume.

Despite the winless record, there was already a movement in the community to get on the pro football bandwagon. The *Press-Gazette* published a four-page advertising section proclaiming support for the Packers organization. The list of organizations included the Rotary Club of Green Bay, Green Bay Elks Club, Advertising Club of Green Bay, and fifteen other organizations.

This was a significant event as it revealed that support for pro football in Green Bay was evolving past the entertainment phase and beginning to attract a financial following. Businesses such as

Schweger Drug, Wisconsin Public Service, The Congress Billiard Room, and Roseman Paper & Supply Company were willing to chip in advertising money in the *Press-Gazette* display. The ads included a promise of better days, words likely written by Calhoun.

> *"In the short space of four years, the Bay has made a name for itself nationally. Its football team is as well known as some of the products manufactured here."*
>
> **- Green Bay Press-Gazette**

"In the short space of four years, the Bay has made a name for itself nationally. Its football team is as well known as some of the products manufactured here. The name 'Packers' under which the team played for three years was a by-word of every football fan in Wisconsin and Michigan. The Packers were supreme and they put football on the map with capital letters. True enough, the home team has suffered reversals in the opening games but it will be a different story from now on."

One popular venue during Packers road games was the Green Bay Elks Club, where fans were invited to show up and hear play-by-play reports sent by Western Union telegraph. A nominal fee was charged for those who wanted to keep up with the game, and fans were told that no score would be flashed outside the building. In fact, Elks Club officials asked people to stop calling the club during the games to check on the score. During one game, more than 500 calls were received. The *Press-Gazette* wrote that "there will be special reservations for the ladies."

Next was a road game to Milwaukee to play the Badgers at Athletic Park. The 0-0 score was virtually hailed as a victory in Calhoun's seemingly endless opening paragraph.

"Fighting like the Packers of old, Green Bay's pro footballers chased the jinx which has been following them all season and Sunday afternoon the scrappy team from upstate spilled the dope by holding the Milwaukee aggregation of All-Americans to a 0 to 0 score in one of the greatest exhibitions of the pigskin sport ever played in this city."

The Monday headline was "Famous Cream City Eleven Fortunate to Escape Loss; Green Bay Displays Class."

Milwaukee's best player was Fritz Pollard, who would become a football legend whose legacy would eventually be recognized when he was inducted into the Pro Football Hall of Fame in 2005.

Pollard tried to kick a field goal during the game, but Jug Earp blocked it. The Packers then drove into Milwaukee territory in the closing minutes to set up a field goal try by Lambeau.

"The oval cleared the mass of tangled players with plenty to spare," Calhoun wrote. "The ball headed straight for the upright but a gust of wind caught it. It miss by less than a foot."

Jug Earp
Packers star and a distant relative of famous lawman Wyatt Earp

Next was a return match against Rock Island, this time to be played at Hagemeister Park. Promotion of the game began immediately. Calhoun, with a possible nudge to Green Bay businessmen, pointed out that the Rock Island community had taken the financial stress off the team management.

"They don't have to worry about such a thing as the almighty dollar," he wrote. "Merchants consider the team an asset to the city and every fall they cut loose the purse strings and tell (team coach) to spare no expense to put a winner on the field. They have their own practice field and are housed in a two-family apartment. They have their own chef."

It was another 0-0 tie, but not without drama.

The referee by the name of Quill drew the ire of Packers fans when he awarded a fumble to Rock Island that fans thought was recovered by the Packers' Gus Gardella.

"He was booed from all sides of the field and was the target of some verbal threats," Calhoun wrote.

According to Calhoun, it was a revenge game for Jug Earp, who had left the Rock Island team earlier in the season.

"Dame Gossip spread some rumors about him in these parts but he squashed them all yesterday," Calhoun wrote, without elaborating. "It seemed as if he took special delight in spilling Jimmy Conzelman, the Rock Island captain."

"Invaders Famous Attack Smashed to Smithereens," read the headline the day after the game.

Walter Flanagan, the Rock Island manager, was quoted of praising the Green Bay team after the game.

"The fighting spirit of the Green Bay team is the best in the country," he said. "From what I have seen and heard, it's like a happy family and take it from me, this is something a bit out of the ordinary with a pro team. We played better football against Green Bay than we did against the Chicago Bears and yet only got a tie game. Unless I miss my guess, the Green Bay club is going to be way up there in first before the curtain is pulled down."

Flanagan seemed to speak in a similar manner that Calhoun wrote.

The crowd was described as boisterous, but it also had a strong racist element. One of the Rock Island players was Duke Slater, a "Negro" from Iowa who took a verbal pounding from Green Bay fans. This sent Kline to his editorial page pulpit.

"Green Bay has built up a reputation of being one of the fairest sporting towns in the country, but poor sportsmanship was evidenced in Sunday's game against the Rock Island club when some of the spectators made verbal attacks on Slater, the Negro tackle of the Rock Island team. Slater has a national reputation on the gridiron. He is known throughout the football world as a class player. Nevertheless, Slater was the target for a number of contemptible attacks. Those who made them ought to be ashamed of themselves and it would be a commendable thing if men who so far forget themselves could be put off the field. The color line is not drawn in football. The remarks hurled at Slater are to be regretted and it is hoped that in the remaining games of the season here Green Bay will live up to its 'play fair' reputation by treating all players alike."

The only people of color in Green Bay were transients or Oneida Indians who had left the nearby reservation. But occasionally, a black man – called Negro then – showed up in town and occasionally ran afoul of law enforcement.

Just a year earlier, two such men were hauled before Judge Thomas Howlett on a charge of shooting craps on a city street.

Said Howlett: "They can't help it. It's born right in them. Why, some of the ebony-hued gentlemen would rather shoot craps than eat chicken, and that's saying a heap."

Political correctness was a development left for the future.

The *Press-Gazette* published a story on its front pages about three Negroes being dragged out of a Texas jail by a mob, lynched, and then burned at a stake. The article concluded, "The lynchings were carried out in an orderly fashion."

Another story about racial conflict in a Florida city contained the headline: Race War in Florida; Two Whites Dead.

The story accompanying the headline indicated that "a score or more blacks are believed slain."

Closer to home, *Press-Gazette* readers were advised that a team from Milwaukee coming to Green Bay to play the Packers included "two colored players, Fritz Pollard and Gene Robeson."

The same month, a report out of Milwaukee disclosed that 300 Green Bay men were registered in the Ku Klux Klan. But, as one letter writer expressed to the *Press-Gazette,* "If you had 300 white-robed Knights of the KKK at your command right here in Green Bay, who would you sic em on first?"

It was the Green Bay Klan members who set out to try and rid the area of the illegal booze.

The Klan's growth in Wisconsin picked up after the war, primarily as a fraternal organization. But soon its targets included Jews, Catholics, African-Americans, recent immigrants, and anyone else it deemed as a radical. It attempted to present itself as a staunch defender of the American way of life. But this was 1922 and racial equality didn't exist in Green Bay.

Gov. John Blaine called the Klan "an organization of hate and hatred," and its presence in the state largely faded away by 1926.

Health was a continued public concern. A year earlier, Green Bay public school officials insisted that all schoolchildren receive smallpox vaccinations before being admitted. This raised a storm of protest from many west side parents, but the School Board prevailed.

City Health Officer Dr. George F. Goggins complained that too many parents were being negligent in failing to get adequate medical help for their children.

"An infant, born to healthy parents, is expected to live more than 54 years," he wrote. "That's 10 more years than a generation ago. If we are to reduce tuberculosis, annihilate typhoid fever and control other diseases, we must apply with greater zeal the knowledge we possess relating to sanitation, hygiene and disease prevention."

Dr. Julius Bellin
(Photo courtesy Bellin Health)

The infant mortality rate in Green Bay was ninety-three of every 1,000 births, a figure that ranked second-highest in the state. Madison, by comparison, had forty-seven deaths per 1,000 births.

There was an outbreak of diphtheria with 186 cases reported and nine deaths resulting in the year. But no smallpox was diagnosed. The Hickory Grove sanitarium south of De Pere had reached its capacity, and Superintendent Emma Rosenbloom said there were hopes of expanding. The facility, built in 1915, was expected to have a capacity of sixteen tuberculosis patients, but was treating forty.

Dr. J. R. Minahan
(Photo courtesy Wisconsin Historical Society)

It was a time of intense medical competition. The leading players were Dr. John R. Minahan who, with the assistance of brothers Robert and Patrick, was most responsible for the continued success of St. Vincent Hospital, and Julius Bellin, who forged the path of what became the hospital and medical system named for him.

Bellin felt excluded from St. Vincent because of J.R. Minahan's dominating presence and control over which operating rooms could be used. Bellin eventually purchased property a block to the north for what became Deaconess Hospital and later Bellin Hospital.

John R. Minahan would gain national notoriety a year later when he removed the heart of an eighteen-year-old girl, held it in his hand while he removed a tack from her lungs, then replaced the heart. The woman survived.

St. Vincent Hospital added an addition in 1927 for laundry service. Dr. J.R. Minahan remained the most influential person at the hospital until his death in 1941.

Medical competition didn't ease up as the decade continued. The Deaconess Hospital added a nurses home and annex in 1923, and the hospital had sixty physicians, surgeons, and dentists using its facilities. The hospital was renamed Bellin Hospital in 1925, reportedly over Dr. Bellin's objections, but he and his wife donated the funds to build a four-story wing that year. Bellin died unexpectedly in 1928.

St. Mary's Hospital was established as a home for unwed mothers and their babies by the Misericorde Sisters of Montreal at the turn of the century on Webster Avenue at Crooks Street. The Sisters began offering medical services a few years later, expanding their hospital several times during the first quarter of the century as well as establishing a nurses' training school.

St. Mary's would remain there until 1960, when renovation of the existing building was deemed impractical and Catholic Bishop Stanislaus Bona requested that a new St. Mary's be located on Green Bay's west side. City officials also were in favor of this move because trains and shipping traffic on the Fox River often prevented west-side emergency services from reaching the existing hospitals.

Interestingly, there was no rush for the hospitals to seek accreditation. St. Mary's was accredited in 1920, Bellin in 1936, and St. Vincent in 1954.

There was scandal in town. Near the end of the month, Register of Deeds Frank H. Smith was arrested after an auditor discovered $1,296.19 missing from the office books. Smith was charged with embezzlement just days prior to the election, helping Rigney Dwyer, the Democratic Party candidate, to victory.

Dwyer was an interesting story. He played for the Packers in the

The Four Horsemen Ride

For the first time, in a game against Georgia Tech, the Notre Dame backfield included Harry Stuhldreher, Don Miller, Elmer Layden, and Jim Crowley. The four would gain fame as the Four Horseman. Crowley was a graduate of Green Bay East High School.

1919 season and part of the following season. But in November 1920, while working at a railroad yard, Dwyer fell under a moving train, lost a leg and had an arm mangled. He survived and had some of his medical costs paid through proceeds from a special benefit football game featuring employees of Northern Paper Mills and Bellevue Ice Cream.

Dwyer's football career was over, but he went on to serve twenty-two years as register of deeds before dying in 1944 at the age of forty-eight.

Jim Crowley's football career was just beginning. The Green Bay East graduate was a freshman on the Notre Dame team coached by Knute Rockne and was already making an impression. He would continue to impress, eventually becoming part of the famed Four Horsemen backfield that led the Irish to college football fame.

Another piece of news that had a potential lasting impact concerned the city's effort to build a new YMCA. The Brown County Board had rejected a proposal that it sell the site of the former courthouse in the 100 block of North Jefferson Street, so the city looked one block farther north. There it was able to acquire three lots that gave it 198 feet of frontage between Cherry and Pine streets. This included a grocery store operated by William Winter, the back of property owned by John Findeisen and John Hummel, and two vacant lots owned by the Lucia brothers. It was a popular time for building a YMCA as many similar communities throughout the state were making the same effort to build one.

A committee, under the leadership of Green Bay Planing Mill President Orris Brightman, was formed to raise $350,000 to build the Y. Joining the campaign were leading Green Bay businessmen, including Austin Cofrin of Fort Howard Paper; Carroll Phenicie of

Columbus Community Club: This 1926 image, taken by Bethe Photography, is the Columbus Community Club at 115 South Jefferson Street. The Club boasted a 3,500 seat auditorium, an Olympic size swimming pool, and a bowling alley. The facility was built for $400,000 and was completed in 1925. Located in downtown Green Bay, the club was converted to Catholic Central High School in 1941 and is known today as the WBAY Building. *(Photo courtesy of Neville Public Museum of Brown County)*

Wisconsin Public Service; Harold Joannes of Joannes Brothers Co.; banker John Rose; attorney Victor Minahan; Dr. Robert Cowles; Judge Henry Graass; and Joseph Conway, president of Hoberg Paper Co. It was the leadership of Mitchell Joannes that saw the campaign raise $425,781 to build the six-story structure.

A brochure was produced to make the case, noting that there were 4,810 boys who could be served by the new facility. Construction began in 1924 and was completed in September of 1925.

"(Green Bay's) assessed valuation is $45,030,551 but the worth of its boys would outweigh the physical wealth by every measure we might use," the pamphlet read. "There is no other city of our importance in Wisconsin today that is so poorly prepared to care for its boys as we are. There is no indoor swimming pool, no well-equipped gymnasium."

Calling the new YMCA "a factory for making citizens," the committee leaned heavily on the consequences of not building the facility.

"The only meeting places offered them is the pool hall," it stated. "Green Bay's greatest problems today are presented in its boys. Court records, school records, home records will fully bear out this statement."

Kline hailed it in his editorials.

"The announcement that Green Bay is to have a YMCA building is the best news of a civic character conveyed to the people of the city in a generation," he wrote. "The neglect of young manhood is the greatest single moral weakness of Green Bay."

At the same time, the Knights of Columbus revealed its plans to build a clubhouse – to be called the Columbus Club – between the Kellogg Museum on Jefferson Street and a filling station located at the corner of Jefferson and Walnut streets.

The building would be multi-purposed, including an auditorium to seat 3,500, a gymnasium and twelve bowling alleys. Some wanted it to include a swimming pool, but that wasn't in the initial plans. It would be completed in 1924, but due the Great Depression was turned over to the Norbertine Fathers in the 1930s. The building was the home of Central Catholic High School – predecessor to Premontre High School and today's Notre Dame Academy – between 1941 and 1955. WBAY-TV, the city's first television station, has operated in the building since, and the lower-level bowling alleys operated as Bay Bowl for several decades.

And the *Press-Gazette*, which had been operating out of a building at the corner of North Jefferson and Cherry streets, announced it planned to build a new plant at the intersection of East Walnut and Madison streets. It would be two stories high with the potential to add a third floor in the future.

Chapter 11

November

Packers Face Financial Woes

Green Bay residents had little time to absorb the YMCA news before a major announcement greeted them. The Wisconsin Hotel Company of Milwaukee announced it was going to build a nine-story hotel at the corner of Adams and Pine streets at a staggering cost of $750,000 ($10.7 million in 2017 dollars).

Green Bay had no shortage of hotels and rooming houses – there were twenty-seven in the city at the time – and the Beaumont Hotel served as hotel of choice for many visitors. But this proposed hotel – to be called the Northland – was something altogether new for Green Bay.

Many of the hotels were old. The Cook's Hotel at Cherry and Washington streets was built in 1874 and had just added running water and telephones in 1916. There was also the Hibernian House on North Broadway, soon to be renamed the Northwestern. Bradley House and the New Freeman Hotel were open on South Washington, and the Columbia Hotel was in the 1100 block of Main Street. It eventually became a manufacturing site of saddles and harnesses.

Movin' on up: Construction men work on the new Northland Hotel at the corner of Pine and North Adams streets. It was considered the city's luxury hotel when it opened in 1924. *(Photo courtesy of Neville Public Museum of Brown County)*

None were in the class anticipated by the prospect of the Northland.

The Northland Hotel eventually cost $1 million to build and opened on March 21, 1924. It became the place to be for galas, proms, and other major events. It was also where visiting pro football teams would stay when coming to Green Bay to play the Packers for decades to come. The hotel was transformed into a mixed use commercial and residential property in the 1970s and renovated into an upscale hotel again in 2016-17.

The month began in promising fashion for the Packers when they defeated the team from Columbus, Ohio, 3-0 at Hagemeister Park. The game was witnessed by league president Joe Carr, a native of Columbus, who gave Calhoun the type of promotion he was seeking.

"Seeing is believing and I take my hat off to Green Bay," Carr said.

"I think it is the greatest football town in the country for its size. It seems to be as if everybody from the urchin on the streets to the gray-haired retired businessman thinks, eats and sleeps football. I've been in the game for about 20 years but never in my football career saw a better display of football spirit and community pride."

The weather was miserable, with rain pouring throughout the game making the field a quagmire. Under rules of the time, a team could recover its own blocked field goal and retain possession, which helped the Packers score their only points, a repeat kick by Cub Buck.

The turnout wasn't very good because of the rain and the Packers lost $1,500 because of it, leaving the team $3,400 in the red. The organization had rain insurance, but rainfall was .01 of an inch short of qualifying for a settlement. One day later, Calhoun reported that club management – of which he was a part – had decided to increase the $1.10 tickets to $1.65, and the $1.65 tickets to $2.20.

> *"Seeing is believing and I take my hat off to Green Bay. ... It seems to be as if everybody from the urchin on the streets to the gray-haired retired businessman thinks, eats and sleeps football."*
>
> ***- NFL President Joe Carr***

The move was a gamble because the Clair brothers had taken a lot of criticism for raising ticket prices a year earlier, but it was clear the financial ends weren't meeting. Because of the war tax, the government took 10 percent of the gate, and officials were paid $150. Player salaries were going up.

Calhoun was unapologetic in the *Press-Gazette.*

"If there are any fans in the city who figure it can be done at the prevailing (ticket) prices, the club management will willingly turn over the organization and let them gain by experience, providing they guarantee to finance the loss themselves," he wrote.

But the response wasn't good. The Packers defeated the visiting Minneapolis team the following Sunday, with fewer than 2,000 fans attending. In Calhoun's words, "Management lost another big slice of dough."

He wrote that it "was the greatest exhibition of post-graduate football ever seen in Green Bay and it was unfortunate that the smallest crowd of the season turned out to witness it."

Minneapolis took a 6-0 lead right before halftime on a 54-yard pass play that Calhoun described as "a break of luck." But Lambeau led a second half rally, first running for a 4-yard touchdown, then passing to Mathys for the other score after pretending that he was going to try a field goal.

That set up a rematch with the Racine Legion, this time in Racine. The Packers were forced to change their signals as Jab Murray, who started the season playing for Green Bay, was now playing for Racine.

The Packers took a 3-0 lead early in the fourth quarter on Lambeau's field goal, but Racine converted a fourth-down pass to set up the tying field goal in the closing seconds. Calhoun lamented it "was tough break No. 123 for the Green Bay team this season."

Calhoun also took a shot at the officiating.

"The teams suffered alike from the punk officiating," he wrote. "Referee Moore seemed lost off the Chicago Cardinals lot. Umpire Larsen didn't do a thing all afternoon while the head linesman must have left his glasses at home because he simply couldn't see an offsides."

The next step was to try to bring the Chicago Bears to Green Bay for a Thanksgiving Day game that was sure to bring a sizeable gate. But George Halas, player and coach of the Bears, said he wanted a $4,000

Teddy Tribute

Former President Teddy Roosevelt had died more than three years earlier, but was still remembered fondly by many who had supported him throughout his political career. One was the Rev. T.T. Phelps, who delivered a speech to the Green Bay Rotary Club praising Roosevelt.

"Roosevelt is the greatest phenomenon America has produced," he said. "He left a gap too big for anyone to fill. He was the friend of every class and partial to none. He had the versatility of the Norman, the fearlessness of the Viking, and the creative genius of the Saxon.

"Toleration was the first law of the Roosevelt democracy. Everyone must respect the convictions of his fellow citizen and allow every man the right to worship as he pleases. When a group seeks to repress freedom, then America ceases to be a free and self-governing democracy."

DeLair's Cafe: In the early 1900s, DeLair's Cafe was considered one of the most fashionable establishments in the Green Bay area. Owned by Packers booster George DeLair, the restaurant was located at 208 North Washington Street. *(Photo courtesy of Neville Public Museum of Brown County)*

---

guarantee to bring his team to Green Bay, and the money wasn't there. Calhoun took umbrage.

"It is impossible to bring the Bears to Green Bay due to the heavy financial demands and, to date, Manager Halas hasn't been much interested in booking the famous Green Bay team in Chicago," he wrote. "However, he may have a change of heart before the season ends."

He didn't.

The Milwaukee team offered to play the Packers, but would only play it in Milwaukee. The Packers turned it down, insisting it wouldn't be fair to the Green Bay fans. After all, traveling wasn't easy for many people.

The hope to remain competitive and survive financially hinged on what Calhoun hoped would transpire in the following month.

"Right now, the main trouble is finances and at the December meeting the magnates are going to try to work out some sort of agreement which the salary limit will be cut down considerably," he

Norma Lookalikes

Moving pictures were becoming more and more popular, so the Grand Theater decided to launch a search for a Green Bay-area girl who most closely resembled actress Norma Talmadge. The contest was held in conjunction with the Association of First National Pictures.

"Let's show the world that Green Bay is proud of its beautiful women," said theater manager Frank Cook.

Girls were invited to send in their pictures and more than 100 were received before Margaret Kidd was chosen as the winner. The theater announced it would send her to the West Coast to try to appear in a movie.

wrote. "Of course, post-graduate football still has some rough travel ahead but the worst is over."

Hardly, for the Packers.

There was still that promise from the Duluth team – which had defeated the Packers 6-2 in September – to play a game in Green Bay late in the season. So the Booster Club, headed by restaurant owner George DeLair, helped organize the game for Thanksgiving Day.

Promotion began in earnest.

"The Green Bay football club has done more to put the city on the sport map than any other organization of its kind," DeLair said.

Dr. Webber Kelly chimed in.

"What a shame it would be if Green Bay had to get along without post-graduate football," he said. "Football is a man-making game and when we see it played, we realize we can't get along without it. Our team is keeping Green Bay in the national eye and we want to stay there."

DeLair enlisted the help of several men – Ed Schweger, Ed Krippner, Earl Fisk, Harold Joannes, Chris Dockry, Bob Lynch, Alf C. Witteborg, Dick Sager, and Frank Basche – to sell tickets at $5 and $2. John Kittell took the case to the Green Bay Rotary Club. He said the season had not been successful financially, so the club was asking every businessmen's club to appoint a three-man committee to help sell tickets.

Ed Schweger, a druggist, beat the drum for the Thanksgiving game.

"I think the least the folks at home can do is flock to the game ... and show the management that Green Bay is behind them in their efforts to give the community big league football," Schweger said.

Said Ray Neugent: "Green Bay's football club is deserving of the support of every citizen. This organization means a whole lot to the city and it is up to the fans to give the eleven a lift."

Kline devoted part of the *Press-Gazette* editorial page to the cause.

"Now the question is, whether Green Bay, having developed football to the extent it has, and made good so far as the creation of a real football team is concerned, is going to retain and maintain it. Like any other successful undertaking, it requires money. The best costs money in everything and football is no exception."

Mayor Wiesner said: "The Green Bay professional football team has given our city considerable national advertising. The post-graduate football, in my opinion, is here to stay and I think Green Bay wants to keep its berth among the big fellows. The problem of financing a team of this caliber is enormous and the weekly salary list climbs higher than the average football fan realizes."

The effort was heroic, but the weather wasn't. Rain on November 29, the day before Thanksgiving, left the playing field a mess. The Packers defeated Duluth 10-0, but there was no other evidence of success that day.

Calhoun called it a "muck-covered gridiron" and accused the weatherman of taking the boost out of Booster Day. It was one of the smallest crowds of the season and, as Calhoun wrote the next day, put club management deeper in the hole.

Chapter 12

December

Baptism

There was one more game to play for the Packers. It was a third match against the Racine Legion, this time to be played in Milwaukee. A crowd of 4,500 came out to watch and this time Green Bay emerged the winner, 14-0 on touchdowns by Eddie Usher and Charlie Mathys. It gave Green Bay the unofficial Wisconsin championship.

It left the Packers with a 4-3-3 record for the season. Four years later, the Racine Legion, the Rock Island Independents, the Columbus Panhandles, and Milwaukee Badgers would fold. The Minneapolis Marines lasted until 1930. The Cardinals play on.

The Chicago Bears, meanwhile, lost a couple games late in the season and Calhoun couldn't restrain himself.

"Probably when the 1923 football season rolls around the Chicago Bears minus their title of Chicago or national gridiron championship will not be demanding $3,500 for their appearance off their home lot," he wrote. "It is strange how one or two defeats can take a team off their high horse so far as the almighty dollar is concerned."

Roadhouse blues: Roadhouses such as this one outside of Green Bay's city limits drew the ire of those who wanted Brown County officials to more aggressively enforce morals of the day, especially as they pertained to dancing. *(Photo courtesy of Neville Public Museum of Brown County)*

Football wasn't the hottest topic in the city as the final month of the year commenced.

Morality was.

The targets were establishments called roadhouses or public dance halls that offered dancing and, although it was only referred to in vague terms, prostitution. Most of the places were located outside the eastern city limits in what was then the town of Preble.

A group of interested citizens, as well as health and social services professionals, formed a committee called the Council of Social Concerns and brought a resolution to the Brown County Board. It sought the board's support in seeking legislation that would give the county authority to regulate these businesses.

Their evidence was a report from an investigator hired to look into the conduct of young people at the establishments.

"There were stories of young girls enticed into drinking moonshine by boys equally young, of long drives on dark county roads, of the pitiful condition of girls just entering their teens as a result of a search for a good time," the report read.

According to the report in the *Press-Gazette*, "Ruses and intrigue that are employed by the youth in obtaining and drinking liquor right in the dance halls astonished the members of the council and nauseated them as the lurid details of these county dances were described."

But the supervisors didn't do anything, first insisting they didn't have the authority to govern the businesses, then tabling a proposed resolution that would have asked the legislature to empower it.

That fired up the Green Bay Ministerial Association, which called for a community-wide effort to, in one pastor's words, "curb the vice which is said to be running rampant in Green Bay and which threatens to undermine completely the morality of the next generation."

The *Press-Gazette* came out blazing. In an editorial, Kline wrote, "It is a peculiar circumstance, to say the least, when we find ourselves in a situation where civic organizations and the churches are compelled to do what is obviously the duty of public officials. It appears the county board of supervisors takes the position that what goes on in road houses and dance halls located outside the jurisdiction of the city is none of its concern. Does the County Board wish to appear that efforts of this kind in behalf of social morality are of no public concern? If it is of no concern to the county authorities, of whose concern is it? Unregulated road houses and dance halls are a disgrace and a nuisance. If we deliberately set out to start boys and girls on the downward path, we could find no better way. The attitude of the county board is difficult to understand."

"Ruses and intrigue that are employed by the youth in obtaining and drinking liquor right in the dance halls astonished the members of the council and nauseated them as the lurid details of these county dances were described."

- Green Bay Press-Gazette report

Civic organizations chimed in.

The 350-strong Catholic Women's Club expressed surprise and disappointment at the board's inaction. The Green Bay Women's Club, with 500 members, passed a resolution urging the legislature to give the county power to control the vice, and expanded the effort to include bathing beaches, carnivals and street fairs. The Women's

Relief Corps also went on record calling for action.

Finally, the ministers agreed to use the Sunday pulpits on December 18 to generate public support for a crackdown.

Rev. T.T. Phelps, at Union Congregational Church, blamed dancing and parents for a morality slide.

"The cheek-to-cheek and ear-to-ear dance is the most brazen, vulgar and grotesque dance that ever came out of the demi-monde," he preached. "Careless and indulgent parents strew the community with virginal wreckage... It is insane of youth to allow their social get-togethers to be turned into spooning parties."

"The cheek-to-cheek and ear-to-ear dance is the most brazen, vulgar and grotesque dance that ever came out of the demi-monde."

- Rev. T.T. Phelps

Union Congregational Church

Rev. T.D. Williams, at St. Paul's Methodist Church, shocked his congregation by disclosing some of the findings of the ministers' investigation.

"The investigation found dance halls and resorts with young women and girls too drunk to dance, stand or sit," he said. "They had lost all power to resist any invasion of the devil. The dance mania has swept the multitudes out of their moral equilibrium. Some of the models are too shocking for description in church."

Rev. A.T. Erickson, of First Baptist Church, said the chief offenders at these places were businessmen and men of high standing in the community, and he said some of the victims were girls under the age of sixteen.

Rev. G.K. MacInnis, at First Methodist Church, said the community was on the way to ruin unless "some brave leader who does not fear the rabble mob will organize the forces of righteousness and demand that our city and county officials enforce the law."

A summary of the message given to parishioners at Grace Presbyterian, printed in the *Press-Gazette*, read: "Sexuality set to music is no more excusable than any other kind of immorality. The only partners who can dance conscientiously to the music of certain kinds of jazz are those who have been united in the bonds of holy wedlock."

A *Press-Gazette* editorial poured shame on the community for allowing these establishments to function, without really being specific about what occurred there.

"Between the activities of the women and the churches it ought to be possible to get something done for the improvement of conditions alleged to exist in the roadhouses and certain amusement places outside the city. It is a misfortune that no official agency of responsibility appears to exist for the correction of these evils. We ought to have a better regard for our young men and women than this.

"Certainly, it will be admitted that the morals and health of young men and women are of public concern. We have innumerable laws of a protective nature designed to promote these ends. Some of them are enforced and others are not. If they are not enforced it is because the authorities evade their duties and because an indifferent public sentiment tolerates the evasion."

The Council of Social Agencies heard from Dr. George Goggins, the city's health commissioner, who relayed the following comment made to him by a county resident who lived outside the city.

"He said, 'If you of the city would keep your riff-raff at home, we in the rural community would get along without disturbance. It is not our people but the scum of the city that comes out to the county dance halls and raise roughhouse.'"

Goggins lectured that the only way to correct the problem was to impose a curfew.

"You can't get them when they go out but pinch them when they come in," he said.

But nothing happened to change things. In fact, when two men stole slot machines from a roadhouse on Cedar Creek Road, law enforcement looked the other way, concluding there was a law against the use of the machines anyway. Sheriff Nic Ryan disclaimed any knowledge of the alleged robbery.

There was plenty going on behind the scenes for pro football in Green Bay. The poor financial outcome from the Thanksgiving Day game drove Lambeau and Calhoun to try to line up a game against anybody for Sunday, December 10. But the Canton team wanted a $4,000 guarantee and a percentage of the gate. The Dayton Triangles wanted $2,500 and half the gate. The Milwaukee team invited the Packers to play there, but offered no guarantee.

So a decision was made to call an end to the Packers' season that included a 5-3-3 record, a sixth-place finish in the eighteen-team league, and the satisfaction of knowing it finished ahead of the other two Wisconsin teams, Milwaukee and Racine.

It was obvious that something had to be done to change the precarious financial position of the team. The impetus was provided by Green Bay businessmen – headed by Andrew Turnbull – who called a meeting for December 7 at the Elks Club. More than 150 men showed up, the result being the forming of a committee to oversee plans to incorporate and sell stock. The assignment was given to Turnbull, Fred Hurlbut, Ray Tilkens, Leland Joannes, and George DeLair.

A second organization meeting was held five days later at the Beaumont Hotel, with forty-two men showing up. This time, serious business was done. A decision was made to create the Green Bay Football Club and sell 1,000 shares of stock at $10 a share.

In essence, it became one of the most important nights in the history of the Green Bay Packers. Attending were: Ben Masse, Ben Kaster, Cecil Baum, Art Geniesse, Gordon Bent, Jay Gould, Curly Lambeau, Joe Nugent, A.L. Counard, Jim Micksch, Andrew Turnbull, Frank Buchhol, Earle Murphy, Dr. R.B. Powers, Arthur Fontaine, Frank Kerwin, John Martin, Jerome North, Harold Joannes, Lee Joannes, John Golden, George DeLair, Ed Dupperault, Fred Hurlbut, Alf Witteborg, Syl Kersten, Fred Garrett, Ken Schuldes, Milton Larsen, Emmett Platten, Joe Kabat, Ed Schweger, Louis Oldenburg, Forrest Plott, George Holz, Ray Leicht, Tom Dwyer, Ray Tilkens, John Kittell, Victor Minahan, Eben Minahan, and Ed Krippner.

The same night, $1,300 was raised as shares were purchased by Kittell, Hurlbut, Lee Joannes, H.V. Joannes, Schweger, Victor Minahan, Golden, Dupperault, Eben Minahan, Witteborg, Krippner, Oldenburg, DeLair, and Turnbull.

The first stockholders meeting wouldn't be held until nine months later at the Brown County Courthouse (when the decision was made to increase the number of shares to 1,500). But, more than any other day

Egg on Their Face

Two young men entered the W.J. Miller roadhouse on Cedar Creek Road in Preble and asked for ginger ale. Mrs. Miller served them, but one of the men asked for an egg to put into his drink. She declined because it meant she would have to leave the bar unattended.

But her telephone rang in a back room and Mrs. Miller went to answer it. When she returned, she found that the cash register had been rifled and all of the slot machines stolen. In all, she estimated she lost $250.

Nothing was done about it because there was a law against the use of slot machines.

in its history, December 12, 1922, saw the true baptism of the Green Bay Packers. And, it could be argued, the baptism of the city.

Kittell outlined the goal.

"It is planned to dispose of the stock to the football fans of the city and in this way to raise enough funds to start off the season with a working capital in the treasury."

Calhoun basked in the fact that the football team came through 1922 unscathed.

"Remember last year when the coaches association took just a drastic stand against professional football in the annual meeting in New York?" he wrote. "The pro gridders stuck to their knitting during the past fall and lived up to every pledge they made. There was no tinkering with the present day college stars and they peddled their own cause without getting into any argument with the collegians."

Calhoun also noted there was pro football interest in Kenosha and Beloit, Wisconsin, and Duluth, Minnesota. He liked the idea because it would increase interest in the sport in the region.

At the same time, college coaches started to debate what many called team conferences on the playing field.

"A convention system consists in a gathering of players behind the line of scrimmage before each formation," one coach explained. "They form a tight group with their heads together and the quarterback gives the signal. This ring-around-the-rosie holds up the game."

The huddle has survived.

The rest of the 1920s decade was good to the Packers. The franchise was officially incorporated as the Green Bay Football Corporation on August 20, 1923, stating in its application that "the Green Bay Football Club failed last year and the present incorporators took over the franchise and now holds same. The other corporation is insolvent and this is the reason we are organizing a new corporation rather than taking over the stock of the former club."

The team did not have a losing record in any season the rest of the decade, finally beating the Bears 14-10 in 1925. Lambeau began signing players who would have a major impact on the team and the corporation. Verne Lewellyen joined the team out of Nebraska in 1924, and Eddie Kotal became a Packer a year later after playing at Illinois and Lawrence College. In 1927, Lavvie Dilweg and Red Dunn came on board.

But it was the addition of the trio of Cal Hubbard, Johnny "Blood" McNally, and Mike Michalske – all who eventually would be inducted into the Pro Football Hall of Fame – that propelled the team to its first championship in 1929. Its 12-0-1 record included a 0-0 tie with the Frankfort Yellow Jackets on Thanksgiving Day. That team played the Bears twice and beat them both times by a combined score of 37-0.

What lay ahead for the city, state and country was uncertain, but Lawrence College President Samuel Plantz, speaking at the First Methodist Church, sounded a warning.

"As long as there is race hatred and as long as one nation, because of fear, continues to arm against another, the world will be the scene of bitter combat and the ears of peace loving people will hear continued rumors of war. Savagery in the most primitive state will dominate in another great war."

Kline remained as *Press-Gazette* editor until his death in 1930. Turnbull, one of the key organizers of the football team's benefactors in 1922, became the incorporation's first president in 1923 and served in that role until 1927. He remained publisher of the *Press-Gazette* until his death in 1960, always insisting that the newspaper refrain from being critical of the Packers for fear the city would lose the team.

George Calhoun continued as sports editor of the *Press-Gazette* for several more years before taking on other newsroom tasks. He also continued serving as publicity director for the Packers until the late 1940s, when he had a falling out with Lambeau and was dismissed. Calhoun died in 1963.

All that happened in 1922 would have a major impact on Green Bay's future. Fittingly, 1923 would start with new Sheriff Jake Geurts dumping 100 gallons of moonshine into the sewers and demolishing forty stills. But his actions did little to halt the production, purchase, and sale of illegal liquor in Green Bay.

For the greater Green Bay community, there was growth ahead in 1923.

A new Chappell School, Fort Howard plant addition, Northern Paper Mill alteration, Main Street bridge, YMCA, Columbus Club, Brown County Motors garage, a new Vocational School, East High School, Northland Hotel, Fairmont Creamery addition, Wisconsin Telephone Company addition, a new *Press-Gazette* building, a Western Lime and Cement Company plant, Odd Fellows Home addition, Bellin Building addition, and at least 150 new residences.

And the official incorporation of the Green Bay Football Corporation.

As the curtain began to fall on 1922, Kline pondered in print.

"To be honest with ourselves, let us subject ourselves to our own severe criticism and thoughtfully weigh our progress," he wrote in a December 28 editorial. "Where we are going depends largely upon where we have been to get where we are. If we have been taking a ride on a merry-go-round year-in and year-out, seeking only those things which amuse and thrill, then we are sure to find ourselves today right where we were a year ago. The mere thought of being so stupid shames us into avoidance of such inane existence. Ridicule begets serious thought."

Epilogue

It was intended to be all about Green Bay and the steps its people took in 1922 to create a face and a personality that would make the community special for them and everyone who followed.

We know the rest of the story, about a city whose name is known world-wide as the prefix to Packers, whose existence is forever tied to a pro football franchise, and whose people continue to be the beneficiaries of something that could never happen today.

What I underestimated when I began this journey of research was the extent to which my life has been connected to the Green Bay Packers, through the people who intro-duced me to it, through a profession that had genetics written all over it, and through memories that may fade but will never dissolve. Key people included:

Victor I. Minahan

(Walter family collection photo)

He was my maternal grandfather who was a practicing attorney in Green Bay in 1922 and a silent partner of the *Press-Gazette* that he helped start in 1915 with Andrew Turnbull and John Kline. He became the newspaper's editor in 1930 and continued in that role until his death in 1954.

But what I discovered through this project was the fact that he was one of the handful of men who invested financially in the Packers on that December day in 1922. He answered Andrew Turnbull's call to help get the football team out of the red. I'm grateful that he let his daughter marry my father.

The family ended its ownership share of the *Press-Gazette* in 1961, six years before I was hired.

John Kline

(Photo courtesy Green Bay Press-Gazette)

The man became the conscience of Green Bay through the editorials he wrote or approved. He died in 1930, but things he did prior to that had an impact on my story. Prior to moving his family into a house on South Madison Street in the early 1920s, Kline lived in a residence at 812 E. Mason Street that was shared by my father, Dad's cousins, and his grandmother.

When my father thought he had to drop out of Lawrence College in 1926, it was Kline who became his benefactor. He paid for Dad's tuition, and his only stipulation was that Dad should pass this generosity on to those in need in the future. It was a promise kept.

Andrew Turnbull

(Photo courtesy Green Bay Press-Gazette)

Aside from Lambeau, he was probably most responsible for the continued existence of the Packers. Whether it was his vision, a need for a pleasant distraction, or just a hunch, Turnbull kept the football team from going the way of the Canton Bulldogs, Columbus Panhandlers, Racine Legion, and Rock Island Islanders.

It was Turnbull, I had been told, who instructed the newspaper's reporters to write favorably about the Packers for fear the city might lose its franchise.

As business manager (later called publisher) of the *Press-Gazette*, he hired my father as the first manager of WJPG radio station in 1946. Dad and Turnbull met almost daily in those early days as the newspaper corporation, which owned WJPG, debated whether to get into the new television market. It didn't.

Turnbull died in 1960.

George W. Calhoun

(Photo courtesy Green Bay Press-Gazette)

His role in the Packers' birth and survival cannot be ignored. As sports editor of the newspaper and publicity director for the Packers for many years, he functioned in an age when conflict of interest wasn't an issue in Green Bay.

The son of the man who helped build the city's waterworks, Calhoun was just thirty-two as the Packers lost, then regained their pro football franchise in 1922.

Calhoun had many newspaper roles through the years, several years as wire editor, and those who worked alongside of him described a grouchy man who was never seen without a cigar in his mouth. He and Lambeau had a disagreement in the late 1940s and Calhoun's role with the team ended. He died in 1963.

John Walter

(Walter family collection photo)

My father grew up in Green Bay and was raised by his grandmother, Flora Clisby, because his mother died giving him birth in 1907. His relationship with his father (G.A. "Gus" Walter) was often strained. Gus was one of the executives of the Hagemeister Brewing Company, but got into trouble in the 1920s when it was discovered that the company was making beer during Prohibition.

Through his connection to Kline, Dad worked summers at the *Press-Gazette*, then landed a full-time job there in 1930 when he graduated from college. These were the early days of the Great Depression, so having a job was coveted.

In March 1935, sports editor Art Bystrom resigned to take a job with the Associated Press, and Dad became his successor. My father kept a daily diary from 1925 until 1959, so I have his thoughts on many personalities and events involving the Packers. My favorite was his entry on September 10, 1935, when he wrote this about a Packers rookie receiver.

"Tonight's Packer feature was on Don Hutson, the All-America end from Alabama who was catching Dixie Howell's passes in the Rose Bowl last New Year's Day, He'll never be a pro all-american ... he can't block and is too brittle ... very fast though."

Just twelve days later, he wrote this about the Packers-Bears game at City Stadium.

"The Packers, playing brilliant ball, defeated the Chicago Bears 7-0 before 13,000 wildly cheering fans. Herber passed to Hutson for a touchdown the second play of the game and Hutson outran the Bear secondary to the goal line. It was an 83-yard gain, and the stands went crazy."

And the following day: "That sensational football victory of yesterday is the one topic of conversation, dwarfing even the impending European war and the Italy-Ethiopia disturbance."

Then, after a 27-0 victory over Pittsburgh, Dad wrote, "Featured was some spectacular pass receiving by Don Hutson, who is the fastest man in pro football."

The best was probably the October 27 game against the Bears in Chicago.

"Trailing 14-3 with but two minutes left to play," the diary reads, "the Packers suddenly went crazy. Don Hutson took a pass and ran 69 yards for a touchdown. Ernie Smith then recovered a fumble on the 13-yard line, (George) Sauer hauled it to the 3-yard line and a Herber to Hutson pass put it over, the Packers winning 17-14."

Hutson played eleven seasons for the Packers, scored ninety-nine touchdowns, averaged 16.4 yards per reception, was greatly responsible for making the forward pass a weapon in the NFL, and was one of the first inducted into the Pro Football Hall of Fame.

Sorry, Dad.

Taking to the skies: The Packers were the first NFL team to travel by airplane to a game. In this 1940 photo on a trip to New York to play the Giants, you can see Packers quarterback Arnie Herber to the left of the stewardess (third row back), and my dad, John Walter, at right looking at the camera. *(Walter family collection photo)*

In 1939, he wrote this:

"Not on speaking terms with Lambeau, which I believe hurts him as much as it does me. The bosses are making strenuous efforts to patch up our differences, which is all right with me."

The same year, prior to the Packers clinching the Western Division title, the league decided that a championship game against the New York Giants would be played in Milwaukee and not Green Bay.

"This will cause a furor in Green Bay, but it is a wise decision. Personally, I have a hunch we never will get in the playoff," his diary read.

Wrong again. The Packers won in Detroit the following week, 12-7, and prepared to play the Giants in Milwaukee.

"The town is seething with dissatisfaction because the playoff game will be at Milwaukee," his diary read. "Think our paper is too conservative in dealing with the situation, but orders are orders."

The Packers beat the Giants for the title, 27-0, and Dad rode on the Green Bay fire truck in the celebratory parade in Green Bay the following day. He also noted that he was given a wristwatch by the Packers at the championship banquet at the Columbus Club three days later.

It was a different kind of relationship between teams and reporters then. His diaries reveal that he often socialized with the players, invited some (Johnny Blood, Don Hutson, and others) to his home for dinner.

In fact, when Dad and friends participated in a scavenger hunt in 1938 and one of the clues required teams to bring a large item, Dad went out and got Buckets Goldenberg, a heavy Packers lineman.

Dad was called into the Army in 1941, then managed the radio station after the war where he hired Earl Gillespie as his first sports director and Blaine Walsh as a news-man. Both men went on to become broadcasters for the Milwaukee Braves baseball team.

Dad took me to home games at old City Stadium beginning about 1953. He had purchased season tickets in the 1940s and our seats at the new stadium dedication in 1957 were commandeered for Vice President Richard Nixon and his entourage. Our family was given seats elsewhere in the stadium, and I ended up in the first row around the 20-yard line ... next to Miss America. I was eleven.

As a Boy Scout leader, Dad had an annual event at Grace Lutheran Church in which veteran scouts would fry fish to help welcome the new scouts. Dad would make arrangements to have a couple Packers players show up at the event.

In 1958, the two Packers who came to the church were running back Jack Losch and a backup quarterback named Bart Starr.

We also had an autographed picture of Hutson hanging on our dining room wall dur-ing my childhood. I don't know what happened to it.

When the Packers won a road game in the last years of the 1950s (which wasn't often), Dad would drive us to the airport to welcome the team.

Dad died in 1959 at the age of fifty-two.

As miserable as those 1950s teams were, they were so spectacular throughout the 1960s under Vince Lombardi. I attended most home games, including the championship games in 1961 and 1965.

I watched Vince Lombardi's first game as Packers coach in 1959 – the win over the Bears – from the field. I had broken my leg during freshman football practice at De Pere High School, so Dad arranged for me to be in a wheelchair at the side of the field.

It wasn't my last time watching a game from the field.

I acquired a part-time job at the *Press-Gazette* in the fall of 1967. My job was to answer the phones on the sports desk. When the Packers qualified for the NFL champion-ship game at the end of the 1967 season, I was assigned to work with a photographer for the Associated Press at the game. My job was to take his film to a dark room under the stands whenever he completed a roll.

This was the Ice Bowl, and shortly before the kickoff, the photographer started pack-ing up his equipment. He told me his camera was frozen so he was going to the hotel to watch the game. I asked him what I should do and he said he couldn't care less.

My game credential required that I stand away from the sidelines and back up against the stands. But who was checking? So I spent the entire game walking along the sidelines, going behind the Packers bench when necessary. The game ended with Starr's iconic quarterback sneak, and I watched it happen as I stood on the west end of the end zone, virtually even with the goal line.

Hired fulltime, I was soon included in coverage of the Packers' games, but my assignment was always the visiting locker room. My first game was against the New Orleans Saints in Milwaukee and, being nervous, I got to the Saints' locker room before the players had come up from the field. After they plodded in, Coach Norb Hecker started his post-game speech to the team as I sat on a bench right in front of him. Monte Stickles, a mean-looking player, was sitting next to me and quietly told me that I should wait outside. I did.

Once I was assigned to cover the Lions' locker room after a game at Lambeau Field. Detroit's ornery defensive lineman, Alex Karras, had been injured in the game and I was told to find out if he planned to play in the Lions' game a few days later on Thanksgiving.

I asked, politely, as Karras sat in front of his locker. He looked up at me and said, "I'll tell you the same thing I told every other reporter who asked me that stupid question." Karras slowly stood up, then quietly said, "I don't know."

Still breathing, I thanked him and walked away.

I never interviewed Lombardi, but I still have a soft spot in my heart for his successor, Phil Bengtson. I had been assigned to cover his press conference at the annual summer media event at Oneida Golf and Riding Club. I messed up the time schedule and when I walked into the room adjacent to the dining room at the club, the press conference was almost over. I began to think my sportswriting career might be brief.

Phil apparently saw me come in late and when the press conference ended, he walked over to me and asked if I had any other questions for him. I got enough for my story, remained employed, and was always grateful to Bengtson.

Promoted to sports editor in 1977, I was blessed with a remarkable staff that included Cliff Christl, Bob McGinn, Jim Zima, Dave Otto, and Don Langenkamp. My job, related to the Packers, was to take credit for everything they did well. Coverage of the Packers had changed under the leadership of my predecessor, Len Wagner. There was no more looking the other way when poor performance dominated, no more riding on fire trucks, and certainly no wrist watches.

I was never a Packers beat writer, but was usually involved in coverage of the home games. I remember going into the Minnesota

Vikings locker room at Lambeau Field in the late 1970s when quarterback Fran Tarkenton was nearing the end of his career. I stopped him as he crossed the room and asked if he could answer a couple questions. He snarled at me and started to walk away. Doing what I never would have done in my earlier days – or with Karras – I told Tarkenton that I was just trying to do my job. He turned and said, "OK, what do you want to know?"

Unlike my father, I never got close to the players or coaches, and never socialized with them. I preferred keeping a distance and so did the reporters who worked with me.

Perhaps my most memorable moments came in the early 1980s when I got word that former Packer Johnny "Blood" McNally was in town. I contacted him at the Beaumont Hotel and he invited me to come over. A dapper dresser and handsome as he neared his eighties, McNally started sharing stories, some which I knew I could never put in print. As we talked, there was a knock on the door and in came ex-Packer Mike Michalske. The two Pro Football Hall of Famers reminisced about times past and I got to listen. A year later, Michalske died. Two years after that, McNally died.

My last interaction with the Packers as a journalist was the Super Bowl in Dallas in 2011.

Few sportswriters today will acknowledge that they hope the team they cover will win. Such admission seems to fly into the face of objectivity. I always wanted to do my job professionally, but I also wanted the Packers to win. Maybe it was because a winning team is easier to cover. But in my case, it was probably more than that.

We have a history, the Packers and I.

Acknowledgements

A roadblock to listing those who should be acknowledged for their contributions to this project is the certainty that some would be omitted because of memory failure by the acknowledger.

But some must be listed here.

Foremost is my mother, Mary, whose respect for and skill with the written word cannot be overstated. She provided the beacon that led to a career and a passion for writing.

Others who stepped in my path to guide, redirect and inspire – even if they didn't know me – are (first names only): John, David, Tom, Len, Bob, Jane, John, Mike, Alan, William, Harper, Mary Jane, and Louise.

Lastly, to my editors and publishers, Mike Dauplaise and Bonnie Groessl of M&B Global Solutions Inc., for helping to make what was not clear to be clear, what was okay to be good, and for sharing our love for all that is Green Bay.

About the Author

Tony Walter
(Jen Lucas Photography)

Tony Walter has been telling the story of Green Bay for generations as a reporter, editor, and columnist for the *Green Bay Press-Gazette* and now in retirement. His beats have included education, politics, crime, government, and human interest. Sports stories dominated much of his career, giving him access to the people who guided the fortunes of the Green Bay Packers.

A native of De Pere, Wisconsin, Walter studied at Lawrence University in Appleton, Wisconsin, and completed his undergraduate studies at St. Norbert College in De Pere, where he graduated in 1969 with a major in English. He served in the United States Marine Corps Reserves from 1966-72.

Walter's journalism journey included an on-field assignment during the 1967 NFL Championship Game, known as the Ice Bowl, and a one-on-one interview in 2008 with Sen. Barack Obama. He also covered the Wisconsin state government in Madison from 1973-76 and was a member of the prototype team for a new publication called *USA TODAY* in 1981.

He received awards from the Wisconsin State School Boards Association, the Wisconsin Teachers Association, and won first place for sports writing by the National Sportswriters Association in 1983.

The father of two and grandfather of six, he has worked in youth ministry for the Episcopal Church for the past thirty-four years.